The Renewal of Preaching in the Twenty-first Century

The Renewal of Preaching in the Twenty-first Century

The Next Homiletics

DAVID JAMES RANDOLPH

With Commentary by Robert Stephen Reid

Second Edition

CASCADE *Books* • Eugene, Oregon

THE RENEWAL OF PREACHING IN THE TWENTY-FIRST CENTURY
The Next Homiletics

Copyright © 2009 David James Randolph; Commentary Copyright © 2009 Robert Stephen Reid. All rights reserved. Except for brief quotations in critical publications or reviews, no part of this book may be reproduced in any manner without prior written permission from the publisher. Write: Permissions, Wipf & Stock, 199 W. 8th Ave., Suite 3, Eugene, OR 97401.

Cascade Books
A division of Wipf and Stock Publishers
199 W. 8th Ave., Suite 3
Eugene, OR 97401

www.wipfandstock.com

ISBN 13: 978-1-55635-974-3

Cataloging-in-Publication data:

Randolph, David James, 1934–

The renewal of preaching in the twenty-first century : the next homiletics / David James Randolph; with Commentary by Robert Stephen Reid.

xviii + 142 p. ; 23 cm. Includes bibliographical references.

ISBN 13: 978-1-55635-974-3

1. Preaching. 2. Preaching—21st century. 3. Preaching—United States. 4. Bible—Homiletical use. I. Reid, Robert Stephen. II. Title.

BV4211.2 R43 2009

Manufactured in the U.S.A.

*This is for you who are called to preach
and those who love you:
Pastors, Teachers, Family, Parishioners, and Friends*

*Let the words of my mouth and the images of our media,
and the meditations of our hearts
be acceptable in your sight,
O God, our strength and our redeemer. Amen.
A Prayer for the Twenty-first Century based on Psalm 19:14*

Contents

	Acknowledgements / ix
	Preface / xi
One	Renewing Preaching in the Twenty-first Century Context / 1
Two	Content and Concern / 23
Three	Connection and Confirmation / 40
Four	Construction and Composition / 57
Five	Communication / 71
Six	Concretion and Transformation / 85
Seven	Conclusion / 104
Eight	Commentary by Robert Stephen Reid / 113
	Bibliography / 139

Acknowledgements

I AM GRATEFUL TO all those who have contributed to this work directly and indirectly. I thank Robert Stephen Reid for his elegant commentary and distinguished scholarship.

I thank David J. Randolph III, my son, also known as David Madgalene, who prepared the manuscript for publication with the touch of the artist.

I am grateful to my colleagues and students at Olivet University in San Francisco, including William Wagner, Ching Cheng Lee, Merrill Smoak, William Willis, Thomas Cowley, Ray Tallman, and especially Joan Carter, who is also a colleague in Berkeley as well as San Francisco. Thanks also to Walker Tzeng, Tracy Davis, Faith Kim, and Lucia Bendzalova. David Phillips deserves special thanks regarding distance learning.

I am grateful to my colleagues and students at the Center for the Arts, Religion and Education and others at the Graduate Theological Union in Berkeley. Dr. Jane Dillenberger enlightens and inspires me now as she has from the beginning in our days at Drew when I began theological study and she began theological teaching.

My undying thanks go to Doug Adams for his leadership and friendship.

I thank Dr. John Thomas Randolph, my brother in more ways than one, for all he has contributed to who I am and my understanding of preaching across the years, continuing into this Internet era.

I thank Tracey, Carlos, and Anthony Ballesteros, and Judy Irwin: my daughter, son-in-law, grandson and daughter-in-law who lovingly keep

Acknowledgements

me in contact with the struggles of the real world and the strength to deal with them.

I am grateful to David Theroux, President of the C. S. Lewis Society of California, for enriching my appreciation of Lewis.

I am grateful to my long time friends in the Academy of Homiletics, many of whom are noted in these pages.

I thank my new friends in communications: Ted Baehr, Ken Wales, Mike Rhodes, Bob Beltz, Stewart Heller, and Jerry Rose.

Now the great cloud of witnesses gather around me: My mother and father, sister Joy and brother Harry; my pastors and colleagues; my teachers, especially Carl Michalson, Stanley Hopper, and Paul Tillich; the people in the congregations to whom I ministered and who ministered to me; the marvelous people I have met along the way.

Special thanks to the students who give me hope for the renewal of preaching in the twenty-first century.

That said, I alone am responsible for this work. I do thank those who gave rights and permissions.

Thanks to Fortress Press for permission to reprint material from *The Renewal of Preaching*, which Fortress first published in 1969.

Thanks to Hanging Gardens Press for permission to reprint material from *The Renewal of Preaching in the 21st Century*, 1998.

Thanks to K. C. Hanson of Wipf and Stock for publishing this new work and especially Diane Farley for editorial guidance.

There are many others to whom I am grateful for contributing to this work and the names of some appear on these pages. So many others contributed to what lies behind it that if I were to name them all it would require another volume. To all of you I say, much love and many thanks.

Preface

A COMMUNICATIONS REVOLUTION IS sweeping through the churches, setting some on fire with enthusiasm and leaving others burned out. This work shows what makes the difference and how that can empower Christian communications locally and globally.

Those leaders and churches that are thriving are part of the renewal of preaching that is growing up with the promise of transforming the twenty-first century. Born amid the revolutions of the 1960's, nurtured in the globalizations of the late twentieth century and disciplined by September 11, 2001 and its aftermath, this new preaching is using emerging media and enduring faith to bring new life to church and community.

The purpose of this work is to explore this phenomenon, consider its sources and prospects, assess its strengths and weaknesses and open possibilities. It is both descriptive and prescriptive. It encourages participation in the renewal and proposes ways to move forward that are intended to provide a basis and framework for further explorations. Many splendid resources unfortunately are not included here because of publication factors and I am sure others will emerge.

The Next Homiletics will combine Deep Faith and High Tech to deepen devotion to God and widen service to humanity. Whether the Next Homiletics will be "Digital or Dialogical," as Robert Reid puts it in his Commentary, is a major question. I propose a renewal of preaching that is both dialogical and digital.

It takes audacity to hope for the renewal of preaching and faith in a century already greatly challenged; but this is precisely what Barack Obama has heralded. On his path to the Presidency of the United States, he addressed the role of Christian preaching in public life more directly

Preface

and forcefully than in any other modern presidential campaign. One occasion for this was his response to criticisms made of him about his association with sermons by the Rev. Jeremiah Wright, who was the pastor of the church in Chicago of which he was a member. In his "A More Perfect Union" speech delivered on March 18, 2008, he gave a ringing affirmation of the freedom of the pulpit and the responsibility of the preacher in the context of racial healing which is already considered one of the truly great speeches. He projected his vision in eloquent oratory, his televised conversation with Rick Warren at Saddleback Church, his book *The Audacity of Hope* (especially chapter 6 on faith).[1]

It is far too early to tell if this hope will lead to renewal. But it is already clear that Obama's vision of the future that propelled him to the Presidency of the United States is deeply rooted in Christian faith and experience, directly connected to congregational life in community, specifically linked with preaching and open to dialogue with other religions, steeped in the oratorical traditions of history and connected to the new media of the network generation. These themes will be explored in this book.

The promise of preaching has never been greater than it is early in the twenty-first century as seen in the signs of hope identified below. Yet the perils of preaching have also never been greater, and, these are faced honestly. This work explores ways to maximize the promise of preaching and confront the perils to the renewal of church and society.

"How shall they see without a preacher?" is as crucial for the twenty-first century as "How shall they hear without a preacher?" was to the first. Ours is a visual age, and we must communicate visually. This requires an appeal to the whole person, as the arts have long reminded us, rather than the substitution of one faculty for another.

Preaching poetically is called for in this setting both because of its visual quality and because it is quintessentially biblical. Narrative preaching will continue to be important especially as it impacts visual storytelling. I once asked C. S. Song, a great theologian of story, how he differentiated poetry from story. Song replied that he considered poetry to be storytelling in its shortest form. That captures the continuity between the two, but there is a critical difference: the poem goes directly to the subject while the story proceeds by delay.

1. Obama, *Audacity of Hope*; "A More Perfect Union Speech" is available online: npr.org; and the Conversation with Rick Warren is available at Saddleback.org.

Preface

Thirty seconds to raise the dead is our challenge where thirty minutes was given our fathers for this task. The "sound bite" is one of the most vilified but essential demands of communication today. We will explore this theme also in these pages and discover that this form is also one of the most biblical.

The urgency of the digital dimension is heightened by the shift from analog to digital for all television in the United States in June of 2009 by Congressional action. The "converter box," which symbolizes this shift, will become a cradle or a coffin, depending on whether the shift from analog to digital is also a shift from copying to creativity. The box will not convert people from one way of life to another, of course; but spiritual conversion can be facilitated by a technical one if we think outside that box. The reaction by the people will be decisive. Those who accept the action as merely the substitution of one device for another are likely to be burdened with a coffin for copies of the works of others. Those who seize the shift in technology as an invitation to creativity will find a cradle for new ways of communication and transformation.

All art now aspires to the digital. Walter Pater said that all art aspires to the musical, but now the digital advances the visual and aural to a nearly perfect state. The church will match this aspiration or face expiration.

Fortunately, there are many signs of hope as we face these and other challenges, and we will identify them. They are people principally—individuals and communities—who are finding the way forward. Yerko Ban stands out. And so does Jeremy Nickel.

I have worked with Yerko and Jeremy and their contemporaries from the perspective outlined in this and my earlier works. The genius of preaching is its eventfulness. What is crucial for homiletics is not so much what the sermon "is" as what the sermon "does." Concern, connection, confirmation, construction and composition, communication, concretion, and transformation are terms that arise in answer to the question, "What does the sermon do?" They describe the event of preaching. These terms are basic in the vocabulary of the homiletics that accompanies this new preaching. With context they serve as guidelines to the plan of this book as the chapter titles suggest. Elements presented in the original 1969 edition of *The Renewal of Preaching* have proven effective and influence ongoing theory and practice, even though some of the theological references have been challenged, and some examples became outdated. I have

Preface

made additions and corrections of my own. Robert Reid sets this in context in his commentary.

However, the Next Homiletics developing here is distinctive from its predecessor in its broader theological base and its wider range of reference and engagement with twenty-first century issues. Anyone who reads this work, and its expressions in *On the Way after 9/11* and *Candles in the Dark, Flames for the Future*, and checks out the digital references, will observe significant changes.

We know that preaching has the power to transform. Today we have many ways to discover and communicate them. We also live in a time of enormous challenges.

What can we do to develop, create, and enable worship and preaching that faces the troubles of our times with a positively transforming power? This is the basic question of this work. Our purpose is to open up possibilities for preaching in the twenty-first century, building on learning past and present.

There are three basic options in this context of the Christian tradition being faced with major challenges. One is to *repeat* what we are now doing and try to preserve what we have inherited. Some believe that the status quo is working for them and intend to keep it going. For others this is a default position in the absence of a serious alternative.

A second option is to *replace* what we now have. This appears in appeals both to the future and the past. Some foresee a radical break with tradition in favor of a technologically controlled spirituality. At the other extreme, the return to the Latin Mass in the Roman Catholic Church, while recent and controversial, is seen as a serious effort to replace the changes of Vatican II for older patterns of worship and preaching.

A third option is *renewal*, which affirms what is central in what we have inherited and now have, and critically expands this with new resources to meet emerging needs. Renewal seeks to fulfill the purpose of preaching by assessing strengths and weaknesses in various options in a quest for the best way to honor tradition, meet present needs, and prepare for the future.

Renewal is the option we believe to be best and seek to show why in this work. Since our purpose is to open up possibilities, we will find a lively and varied group of passengers. We will find preachers beginning their studies and their elders who are always eager to learn more and preach more effectively. Those who teach preachers will be there, includ-

Preface

ing teachers of homiletics, of course, but also worship, communications, missions and related fields. Lay people will be riding with us. After all, they are active participants in worship and preaching with a large role to play. Also, many of them are lay preachers who want to do their best. Along the way we will surely be joined by all kinds of people, some of who will raise critical questions and others who will bring great inspiration. Expect entertainers and educators, saints and sinners in the crowd.

Since the destination of the ride of this book is the renewal of preaching in the twenty-first century, we must make a number of stops and deal with critical issues.

Beginning with review of the situation today, we proceed step by step through the preparation and presentation of the sermon leading to transformation. The sermon in the local parish is seen as the microcosm of the macrocosm that is the communication of God's good news. We must review the cultural context in which we work. We must stop to be sure that the content, the message that we have to deliver, is secure.

A station is required to consider how this message is connected with and confirmed. Another is required to deal with how the message is to be composed or constructed. Another is required to deal with how we communicate the message.

We must be sure as we reach the end of this route to see how the renewal of preaching connects with the concrete realities of the lives of our passengers so they may go forth in mission to transform. For renewal is a journey, as well as destination, and, ours is a trip to transformation.

A Personal Pilgrimage

When I was young, my father became seriously ill. The doctors gave up on him, but our minister did not. That minister was Edward L. Hoffman. Ed Hoffman counseled and prayed with my father, and my father recovered. This minister revealed the source of this healing power in the sermons that he preached in the little village church where he was a theological student pastor. They brought God and the Bible near to us in Jesus Christ. When Pastor Hoffman invited members of the congregation to follow Jesus Christ, I accepted that invitation.

That has made all the difference.

About this time, I was nearly killed by a bull on the farm where we lived. I wondered seriously why I was alive rather than dead after this near death experience. Also, about this time, Mr. Hoffman invited me to preach the sermon at a youth service. I decided to preach on Psalm 8: "What is man that God cares about us?" The experience of looking over the big Bible on the pulpit, and, seeing the faces of the congregation looking at me expectantly hoping I could connect them with the message through my sermon overwhelmed and thrilled me. It dawned on me that this was why I was alive and not dead—to share this message. I was eleven years old. Preaching was something I was called to do in response to God's word and human need. I did not think of it as a profession until years later. The profession I dreamed of then was to be a big league baseball player, like Lou Gehrig, as depicted in "The Pride of the Yankees."

After that first sermon, I was invited to preach at youth services. Eventually, while in High School, I preached regularly in a chapel in the country to which I would ride my bicycle.

I had no idea then that riding my bike to preach at a country chapel would lead me one day to New York City and around the world. I made it to New York, not as a Yankee but as the Senior Minister of Christ Church United Methodist on Park Avenue. Along the way, I was a pastor in inner cities and suburbs, I preached and lectured in churches, large and small, across America and in Europe and China, was invited to teach at great centers of learning, served as a denominational executive, shared the dream of Martin Luther King Jr. in the March on Washington, and later in Selma. Currently I work with a new generation in the San Francisco Bay area of California on the Pacific Rim. The invitation to faith is an invitation to adventure.

This new generation with which I am now engaged brings with it a passion to communicate that connects with my generation, and me, more than any factors of age, nation, or skills, which might separate us. Consider Yerko Ban, who came to our class at the Graduate Theological Union from his native Croatia. Yerko brought with him a burden to minister to the deaf and blind that suffer from Usher Syndrome. This condition afflicted Helen Keller as millions discovered in the film "The Miracle Worker," and it is still a medical problem.

Yerko was taking on a challenge of biblical proportions. In the Old Testament, the day of the Lord is prophesied when the ears of the deaf are unstopped and the eyes of the blind are opened. Jesus performed this miracle as recorded in the Gospels.

Preface

Yerko believed that the Gospel still has the power in the preaching of the Word and the Sacraments to meet this challenge and that New Media could help communicate this message. I affirmed Yerko in his mission, and the class supported him in his experiments. These were not always successful, as he would admit, but Yerko persisted, identified strengths and weaknesses, made improvements, and moved toward his goal. Yerko worked with his Roman Catholic community, and others, to produce resources to minister to this deaf-blind population, including a website and a video demonstrating a sign language for worship. He also produced a short documentary film on this work entitled *The Vricino Brothers*, which was shown on Croatian National Television. His work came to the attention of a major foundation in Stockholm, Sweden, and is now part of a global movement for education and healing.

This miracle is taking place thanks to the power of God, the vision of a student, and a community of faith and scholarship who believe that power can be facilitated by New Media to fulfill the ancient prophesy that the eyes of the blind shall be opened and the ears of the deaf shall hear.

For me, this connects with the experience of my youth when a pastor brought home to our family the healing power of the Gospel. It is a recent expression of that power that I have witnessed throughout my life and ministry and only grows more marvelous in the face of new challenges.

For all of us, this connects us with that dawn of preaching described in Luke where Jesus returns to his childhood home in Nazareth and reads publicly:

> The Spirit of the Lord is upon me, because he has anointed me to preach the Gospel to the poor; he hath sent me to heal the brokenhearted, to preach deliverance to the captives, and recovery of sight to the blind, to set at liberty them that are bruised, to preach the acceptable year of the Lord.

Then Jesus closed the book and said, "This day this scripture is fulfilled in your ears."

The call to preach is a call to adventure.

The work with Yerko, and others we consider here, are signs and wonders of Deep Faith working with High Tech to deepen devotion to God, and widen service to humanity. They bear witness to what is happening around the world and testify to the potential of what is yet to come.

One | Renewing Preaching
in the Twenty-first Century Context

IMAGINE A TIME WHEN people in large numbers find the purpose of their lives in loving God and their neighbor as themselves. When people reach out to bring peace and justice to all. When people all over the world celebrate a person who lived to the glory of God and the service of humanity. This may seem like a Utopian dream, but it was reality in the spring of 2005 when *The Purpose Driven Life* by Rick Warren was a runaway bestseller, a group led by Jim Wallis and others initiated a new movement for peace and justice in the spirit of Dr. Martin Luther King Jr., and the life of Pope John Paul II was celebrated all around the globe. Women, youth, elderly and others of all races and ethnic backgrounds around the world were less known but no less contributive to this reality.

Whether this moment becomes a memory or a preview of our destiny hinges upon how well the passion for preaching that motivated these leaders and movements is expressed. Whatever their differences, all have in common the commitment to preach the Gospel of Jesus Christ in order to increase love of God, self and neighbor. Preaching here refers generally to the communication of the Gospel and specifically to proclamation in the homily and liturgy. Preaching is not their only activity, but it is the focal and fruitful act fundamental to their leadership in church and society.

"The Primacy of Preaching" is affirmed by all of them and stated explicitly by Rick Warren: "Preaching seems to go in and out of style in many denominations. In our high-tech world, it is often criticized as being an outdated and uninteresting mode of communication. I agree that many preaching styles that once worked no longer effectively communicate to nonbelievers. In terms of seeing radical life changes in individuals, however, nothing else can take the place of Spirit-Anointed preaching. The message is still the most important element of a seeker service."[1] Warren continues to demonstrate the relevance of this claim to society as well as individuals.

To fulfill the promise of preaching we must find its power and face our problems.

Heritage

Emergence of the new brings greater appreciation for the old. The rise of visual media, for example, has broadened the importance of the written word rather than reduce it as many feared. Virtually nothing can move onto the screen without words written as script or direction. And the preachers most effective in using television such as Rick Warren and Joel Osteen have multiplied their ministries through books.

Profound appreciation is due those who at present and in recent years have held high the banner of preaching in difficult times. I think often of an incident in the life of my distinguished seminary professor of homiletics, Henry Lyle Lambdin. One night, while Dr. Lambdin was preaching, the electric lights in the chapel suddenly went out. With characteristic dignity, he continued the sermon, and when the lights came on again Dr. Lambdin was still at his post.

In recent years, persons have often found themselves preaching in the dark. The spotlights that bathed preachers in some other eras have shifted to different places. Yet noble bands in these days have been lights shining in the darkness. These pastors and teachers have shown that the vitality of preaching does not depend on popular approval. It is largely to their credit that as the lights come on again so much residual strength is to be found in preaching.

To be sure, the preachers themselves called down some of the darkness that descended on the pulpit. When preaching is seen as a single act, isolated from the whole responsibility of a pastorate, or when it becomes a means of self-aggrandizement, or when it becomes empty chatter, then it deserves eclipse. Preaching is luminous when it is carried forth as the fundamental, focal, and fruitful act of Christian faith.

---

1. Warren, *Purpose Driven Church*, 306.

The Fundamental Act

Preaching is the generating source of Christian faith. Paul struck the mark when he declared, "Faith comes by hearing" (Rom 10:17). Martin Luther burnished that mark, making it a hallmark of the Reformation: "Faith is an acoustical affair." There are many activities of the church without which it would be defective, but without preaching the church would be defunct.

The Focal Act

The contemporary minister is so besieged by demands that it is easy for him or her to lose sight of what is central. Preaching, in a way unparalleled by any other of the traditional "offices," abides as a focal point for all the work of the ministry. In the preparation and presentation of the sermon, the concerns of teaching, counseling, liturgy, community responsibility, and administration, converge. In preaching, the varied interests of persons and church are drawn to a point, and given direction. For this reason a person with "fuzzy" sermons is likely to have a distorted view of his or her whole pastoral task.

The Fruitful Act

Preaching demonstrates the truth of the words, "You will know them by their fruits." Fruitful preaching is consequential, productive of results. *Time* magazine carried the story of a man who willed his eyes to an eye bank as the result of a sermon he heard; those eyes later brought sight to another. This is a parable of preaching with consequences. When a person gains new perspective on a problem, or when the eyes of a congregation are opened to social responsibility, the sermon has given new eyes to the blind. The sermon is then likely to bear fruit in the personal, and communal, life of the hearers.

Challenge: Preaching Prow or Poopdeck?

Preaching is the prow of the world, declared Herman Melville in *Moby Dick*: "What could be more full of meaning? For the pulpit is ever the earth's foremost part; all the rest comes in its rear; the pulpit leads the world."[2] The passage that describes the sermon of Father Maple on Job comes early in

---

2. Melville, *Moby Dick*, 47.

the novel, and is a clue to the work as a whole. Melville took preachers and sermons very seriously in his struggle with faith.

The Christian pulpit is the prow of the human ship leading into the future, but it easily becomes a poopdeck bringing up the rear. Melville's metaphor resonates today as we see preachers who are superb communicators in vital churches and ministries in loving service to the world mentored by wise teachers in great centers of learning. However, there are some churches where the minister simply mouths words from sermons from some Internet service in parishes that are themselves adrift, as well-meaning seminaries ill-prepare their students for the twenty-first century.

Whether the pulpit shall be prow or poopdeck is of vital concern not only to preachers but also to the churches, the community and the culture.

Look Around

Leonard Sweet seizes the relevance of the aquatic imagery used by Melville with his invitation to get the church seaworthy and seagoing again, to rediscover the vocation of voyaging. Contemporary culture is fluid rather than fixed as we see in relationships, creeds, technology and politics, Sweet argues, and leaders must prepare new ways to navigate these waters. One of the books in which Sweet spells this out is entitled *Aquachurch*. An ironic affirmation of Sweet's claim is that the flow of events has outpaced some of his postmodern philosophical references. Post 9/11 better describes our situation than Postmodern, but Sweet's orientation to the "SoulTsunami" culture of the new millennium is to be taken seriously.

While preaching and churches do not control culture, they contribute to its health or illness. Therefore the renewal of preaching must be considered in relation to the renewal of church and society. Therefore the rise of violence and the clash of cultures must be addressed.

Homiletics as the discipline that guides preaching for decades was regarded as the preparation and delivery of sermons. This must be expanded if preaching is to deal with the emerging situation. While preparation remains basic, homiletics must deal with communications more broadly to be effective in a media age, and, it must show how faith impacts social as well as personal crises. Renewal of preaching in the twenty-first century will deal with the preparation, communication and transformation of sermons. Visual art studies, especially film, will take its place with rhetoric as resources for preaching and worship.

Within this fluid context there are defining elements. We will note them here and deal with them more fully later. Briefly they are:

1. Christianity is growing significantly around the world.
2. Challenges are serious.
3. New Media and electronic technology offer an equally enormous opportunity for communication of the Christian message and transformation of society.

We will develop these themes throughout but note the dialectical relationship between these factors of thesis, antithesis and synthesis as historical as well as rational.

Christianity is growing significantly around the world. This trend is overwhelmingly clear, although statistical and anecdotal evidence varies. Christianity is the world's largest faith community, and it is increasing in size and scope. This growth is rapid in some areas, such as Africa and Asia. Statistics show a decline in church membership in Europe and North America, but these statistics relate to traditional membership in mainline denominations. Considerable evidence shows that new forms of worship and mission are adding to the Christian movement in North America. It is coming in the face of competition with other faiths and worldviews, largely from persons who are persuaded that the claims of the faith are not only true, but also powerful and totally relevant to their lives. This growth must be taken not only as a social statistic, but also as support for the central claim that in Jesus Christ, God meets people in their deepest needs and highest hopes as Creator, Redeemer and Transformer.

Challenges to Christianity are serious and increasing. The rise of Islam, and other world religions, and the persistence of an atheistic secularism in a world of increasing violence, and poverty, must be dealt with creatively, now. The most profound change from the late twentieth century to the early twenty-first century context is summed up in the term Post- 9/11. This refers of course to the September 11, 2001 attacks on the World Trade Center, and elsewhere, and their aftermath.

The defining element of the cultural climate in the first decade of the twenty-first century is Post 9/11. Virtually everything is referenced by the attacks on the U.S. on September 11, 2001: after 9/11, or since 9/11.

Postmodern, Post-Christian and other "posts" still stand, but it is the 9/11 that describes the large cultural and small personal shifts that we are still undergoing.

An example of this shift for the church is evident in Trinity Parish Episcopal in New York across the street from the World Trade Center. In June of 2001, I worshipped there, and, heard the Rector Dan Matthews in his sermon describe the challenges facing the church. As I recall, he had recently attended a denominational Board meeting at which the Board had struggled with what they were to do with the surplus of millions of dollars in their accounts. I confess to feeling a touch of envy, since problems like that I never had. However, it was no joke. The church was struggling with problems of surplus. It is hard to believe now but that was a real problem in America in the late 1990's.

I was not able to worship again at Trinity Parish until months later, but the church was still closed for repairs from 9/11, and we had to worship in St. Paul's church nearby. The struggle was no longer with surplus but with deficit—how to make up for all that had been lost in life and treasure by the disaster across the street. The shift from the problems of surplus to the burdens of deficit sums up what is meant by Post 9/11. This applies not only to Church Boards, but the whole U.S. economy, and is symbolic of the sense of shock and loss, not only of lives and buildings, but also of faith and hope still felt by so many, and, which has only deepened with the War in Iraq.

The leadership and people of Trinity Church were heroic in their response, and we can learn much from them, but there are many aftershocks that still define our time.

I have written about this in two other books, *On the Way* and *Candles in the Dark, Flames for the Future,* and will simply note here some major elements in this time of the shaking of the foundations. These include the rise of fear vs. faith, doubt vs. belief, despair vs. hope, war vs. peace . . . the list is all too easily extended. The bottom line is overwhelmingly one of loss.

This loss must be addressed in the preaching and worship of the twenty-first century by a deeper faith that sees that the shaking of the foundations of heaven and earth may lead to another way of Life, whose foundations cannot be shaken, whose builder and maker is God.

President George W. Bush and his administration used religious language in an attempt to support his policies to an unprecedented degree and left behind a burden for politics and theology. Whereas presidents such as Washington, Lincoln, and Franklin D. Roosevelt, referred to the divine on occasion, Bush made such references throughout his career, and, as President he virtually defined himself in terms of his perceived theological mission. Peter Singer documents this in his book *Bush: The President of Good and Evil.*

After the Bush presidency, the basic vocabulary of Christian faith will be burdened by the political uses to which Bush has put it. All citizens will have to decide whether they wish to continue to bear this burden, or cast it aside as an aberration. For the church it is imperative that the hermeneutics of suspicion that characterized much biblical study of the twentieth century be applied to the language of politicians and the media who cover them.

We need a secular homiletics to scrutinize all who would speak from the Bully Pulpit of the presidency.

To do theology Post 9/11 calls for three steps. One is to uncover examples of the political use of religious language to support government policies and politics. Two, is to recover the original, authentic use of the language at its biblical or historical roots. Three, is to discover contemporary ways to relate theological language to political issues in a responsible way.

New Media

New Media and technology offer enormous resources to communicate the Christian faith and to meet the challenges to faith and culture—and more. The most visible signs of this are screens in worship centers and computers in hand, but with World Wide Web and wireless the effects are everywhere.

Just as Post 9/11 presents enormous challenges, New Media offer enormous resources for meeting these challenges and moving beyond them. The rapid growth of Christianity around the world cannot be accounted for by new means of communication, but it would hardly be possible without it. It is also true that opponents of Christian faith have learned how to use these media to devastating effect. A major factor in the twenty-first century will be New Media.

Jeremy Nickel stands out as an individual and representative. He rode into seminary on his motorcycle with long hair flying in the wind. Early in our class, I was more fascinated than impressed. Jeremy wanted to be a filmmaker theologian, and he had unusual personal gifts, with a background in a family oriented to media education. Jeremy was impressed with the spirituality he found in the music clubs in the Bay Area, and wanted to capture this on film. For our class he made a short on the subject that was later made into a feature film called "Sacred Spaces." Jeremy also shared his enthusiasm and knowledge with others in the class, as well as out, and contributed to the growth of our media program by demonstrating how an excellent film can be created with lots of imagination and little money.

Mr. Nickel is my answer to Dr. Dollar. Dr. Crefflo Dollar, that is, of great television fame for his prosperity Gospel to which he feels God called him by having him born as a "Dollar." One could employ that same logic to say that God has called Jeremy to demonstrate what can be done with low budget productions by having him born as a "Nickel." In fact, Jeremy has named his company "Five Cent Films."

The work of Mr. Nickel and his cohorts is as important for the church in the twenty-first century as the work of Dr. Dollar. That may sound ridiculous at the moment because the proponents of the prosperity Gospel are so—well—prosperous. However, with that prosperity comes distortion and danger. Meanwhile, working largely in the dark and known to small numbers of people are revolutionaries who are sharpening a vision of ministry that is destined for a large audience because it requires more creativity and less money and thus is within reach of virtually everyone.

There are two equal and opposite errors the church can make here. One error is to ignore such folk and the other to idolize them. If the church ignores them and minimizes their importance and scorns those who use the New Media, it will become like those porches on the old houses of seamen called Widows' Walks where those at home look vainly for those at sea.

Those at sea will meanwhile be heavily into wireless as pirates if not preachers. The technological trend is irreversible.

The other big error is to idolize New Media, and its proponents. Media, new or old, cannot save us. High tech cannot atone for deep sin. "Conversion" must refer to more than the box that relays the digital signal. Repentance is called for. We must become aware of the abuses we have committed with media and find ways to do better.

Renewing Preaching in the Twenty-first Century Context

Robert S. Reid points out temptations of preaching in the media age that I believe become even more seductive with New Media.[3] While constructive in his approach, Reid identifies six major problems and how to deal with them. These problems are Inauthenticity, Greed, Exploitation, Self-Absorption, Trendiness, and Self-Righteousness. Faithfulness to the Gospel and respect for listeners lead us away from these temptations.

"New Media" refers to media with a digital rather than analogical base, including video, audio, and text, etc., and employing computers and electronic technology, especially the Internet Web 2.0. With reference to art, the term is "time-based," allowing for film and television. New examples continue to appear. New Media are not just media proliferating, but being used synergistically and collaboratively to discover and create new ways of communication, education, commerce, art, entertainment, and human relations. New Media offer new strengths and those are emphasized in this work while not avoiding their weaknesses.

The most visible change in the worship setting for preaching in recent years is the addition of a screen or screens for projected images. Their importance is out of all proportion to the size they take up because they alter the whole process of perception and participation. With them the preacher can now show what before he or she could only talk about.

I found churches on fire with enthusiasm while others were merely burned out when I drove from New York to California to begin a new teaching assignment. Looking for what made the difference, in every church that was thriving I found *screens*—big screens in the worship centers to show projections and live video feed with close-ups of the pastor, etc.; smaller screens on computers in the church offices connecting pastor and people. Screens of every size carrying the service to different venues. The screens made an objective difference in connecting electronically worlds that had been separate; but more than technology, these screens were sacramental: the outer and visible signs of inner and spiritual passion to communicate the message.

Within this context we look more closely for signs of hope and signals of distress.

---

3. Reid discusses these ethical failures of preaching in an Academy of Homiletics essay in 2002: "Irresponsible Preaching," and notes them in another essay: "A Rhetoric of Contemporary Christian Discourse."

Signs of Hope

Christianity is growing dramatically around the world and preaching with traditional worship and emerging media are integral to this expansion. Dr. Ralph Winter of the U.S. Center for World Mission documents his claim that, while some may dispute details, it is indisputable that the overall trend is that biblical faith is growing as never before in history.[4]

There are significant variables such as the rise of Islam, the exception of Europe, and worship attendance versus spirituality.[5] George Barna covers and comments helpfully on the role of emerging media and technology in worship and church life with updates at The Barna Group at www.barna.org.

Preaching as a Force in Social Change Is Being Increasingly Recognized

We find this across the whole theological spectrum. It was the "liberals" who established the validity of the churches addressing social issues early in the twentieth century. Then the "conservatives" became more vocal and powerful. Now there is growing agreement across the whole church that issues such as the war, environment, and poverty belong on the church's agenda. Of course how that is to be done is controversial. Further, the extent to which the agenda will be met remains to be seen. Yet the fact that there is such an agenda is a major shift from the sharp divisions of the recent past.

Scholarship in Homiletics Is Ascending

Since the 1960's, there has developed a treasury of homiletical and liturgical riches greater than at any time since the Protestant Reformation. The emergence of homiletics as a discipline of high scholarly standing is one of the great stories of the church and academy in this period.

This emergence may be traced in the development of the Academy of Homiletics, the leading professional society of teachers of preaching. When Donald Macleod, William Thompson, and I founded the Academy at Princeton, New Jersey, in 1965, a handful of scholars responded. When the Academy celebrated its fortieth anniversary in Williamsburg, Virginia,

---

4. See *International Journal of Frontier Missiology (IJFM)*.
5. See Barrett and Johnson, *World Christian Trends AD 30–AD 2200*.

in 2005, membership was nearing two hundred, and people came from all over the world, bringing wit and liveliness to the meetings. The maturing of one generation of scholar-teachers and the rise of another is evident in the quality and quantity of literature and online activity.

Signals of Distress

Renewal of preaching is by no means a certainty in spite of encouraging signs. There are also distress signals.

Communications Are in Crisis

Today big media often present trivia as if it were gospel while churches present the Gospel as it if were trivia. For example, "Breaking News" appears with flashing graphics and high volume to announce a troubled celebrity shopping at a mall. Sadly, many other examples are easily found treated, trumpeted, and teased to reveal that a mother lied to get her daughter tickets to a concert. Or the *Moment of Truth* program that had barely enough truth to last a moment. Churches on the other hand may be found offering ceramic birds representing faith in return for a donation to support costly programs. The church needs new ways to connect with people and New Media can help. New Media appeal because of their wide reach and lower cost but they should be entered into with full awareness that the communications field itself is in crisis and offers no ready-made solutions for the church that has its own work to do.

Trivialization of the Christian Message Is a Serious Danger

Never has the church had more communications media at its command and seldom has it been so uncertain of the message it has to communicate. This is the downside of media revolution but it cannot be blamed entirely on that. The highly acclaimed "ecumenical consensus" of recent years of Faith and Order has passed and nothing has taken is place. Lectionary usage has assured a selection of biblical texts for preaching but not a coherent faith to hold them together. The success of the Gospel of Prosperity preachers is a glaring example of an alarming lack of substance in preaching.

The Renewal of Preaching in the Twenty-first Century

The Phantom of the Pulpit

The Phantom of the Opera is a character that appears on stage from time to time then disappears to nurse his wounds. There are some distressing signs that he has a counterpart in the church. By this image I want to draw attention to the need of the preacher to be a real person with real needs that must be addressed individually and collectively. Preaching is not merely a role but a vocation. No speaking skills or communications media can long mask the lack of genuine commitment and spiritual practice.

The Next Homiletics and Recent Developments

The Next Homiletics developing here is distinctive from its predecessor in its broader theological base, wider range of reference, and engagement with twenty-first century issues. Many elements presented in the original *Renewal of Preaching* have proven effective and influence ongoing theory and practice, even though some of the theological references have been challenged and specific examples outdated. I have made additions and corrections of my own. Robert Reid gives the context in his commentary at the end.

Paul Scott Wilson writes that the student of preaching today finds "that not since the Middle Ages or the Reformation have such mighty winds swept the homiletical highlands."[6] Change is seen everywhere from the theological understanding of preaching to the forms of sermons to changes in society at large including mass media and computer technology.

In commenting on changes in preaching, Wilson writes:

> Toward the beginning of this shift to experience, four claims were made for the renewal of preaching that have since proved to be foundational for contemporary homiletics:
>
> 1. The sermon ... proceeds from the Bible as God's word to us and connects with the situation of the hearers; it does not arise from religion in general and address the universe.
>
> 2. The sermon moves fundamentally to *confirmation* from affirmation, rather than to evidence from axiom.
>
> 3. The sermon seeks *concretion* by bringing the meaning of the text to expression in the situation of the hearers, rather

---

6. Wilson, *The Practice of Preaching*, 12.

Renewing Preaching in the Twenty-first Century Context

than abstraction by merely exhibiting the text against its own background.

4. The sermon seeks *concretion* by bringing the meaning of the text to expression in the situation of the hearers, rather than abstraction by merely exhibiting the text against its own background.

Wilson identifies the source of these claims "that have since proved to be foundational for contemporary homiletics" as the earlier edition of the present work (pp. 22–23). That statement quoted marks the first appearance in book form of the approach that I had developed in parishes, in Graduate Studies at Boston University, and in lectures at Drew University where I was teaching. It was also presented in a lecture at the founding meeting of what was to become the Academy of Homiletics at Princeton in 1965.

Paul Wilson's book is a landmark amid those mighty winds, summing up much that was valuable and suggesting more to come. I am grateful for the opportunity to contribute to this historic movement. Not everyone has been so affirmative but I am grateful also to my critics who have broadened the discussion. In the years since it first appeared I have tested it in many settings from the Forest in New Jersey to Park Avenue in New York across America and around the world and now as I continue teaching on the Pacific Rim in California. Out of all this, I have found that the foundation noted by Paul Wilson is firm but more is called for.

The Next Homiletics, the homiletics that is emerging in the twenty-first century, will build on the foundation secured in the twentieth century in its theological seriousness and communications creativity. It will continue in its concern for biblical message and human contact, seek connection and confirmation, be concrete, and seek effective construction and communication. Its goal will be eventfulness. In addition, it will develop new resources to meet new challenges.

The Birth and Rebirth of Homiletics and Preaching

The words "homily" and "homiletics" are derived from the Greek *homileo* as it appears definitively in Luke 24:14–18. The setting is the conversation between Simon and Cleopas on the Emmaus Road to from and to Jerusalem. They are talking passionately about the things that have been happening around Jesus of Nazareth whom they believed to be a prophet and redeemer in the tradition of their Scripture. He had just been crucified. A stranger joins them as they walk and he interprets the Scripture in such an illuminating way that they invite him to stay and have something to eat. As the visitor blesses and breaks the bread, Simon and Cleopas suddenly realize that the stranger is none other than their Lord, who vanishes. Recalling how their hearts burned within them when He opened the Scriptures as He walked and talked with them along the way, they race back to Jerusalem to declare that He has indeed risen and appeared to them.

As they are reporting this to the ten disciples gathered in Jerusalem, Christ appears affirming what Simon and Cleopas had said and commissioning them to preach repentance and forgiveness of sin to all nations, beginning in Jerusalem. After Jesus blesses them, they felt great joy and continually blessed God in the temple and out.

When they carry out this mission, other words are used for preaching, including *keryx* for herald, to proclaim and *kerygma* for the message proclaimed. Note Luke's use of this root word in Jesus commission in Luke 24:7, as well as in Acts. Other words may be used for preaching but when authentic they retain the meaning of *homileo* in the encounter at Emmaus and its aftermath.

Based on this origin, a homily is a passionate conversation relating the things that matter most to the Bible in which Jesus Christ becomes present in a transforming way. Homiletics is the study of this phenomenon for the purpose of fulfilling Christ's commission to preach repentance and forgiveness to all the nations beginning at home.

This account of the birth of homiletics is critically important because the rebirth of homiletics in the twenty-first century depends on recovering this distinctive dynamic.

Preaching is the highest form of human communication because it offers the divine message through human means. The manifestation of this preaching is therefore unique although it means of expression are not. The uniqueness of the sermon lies not in what it is but in what it does. The sermon is *sui generis*, one of a kind, not because of its form but because of its function. Homiletics, the study of preaching, is unique and not just a branch of rhetoric because of this theological dimension.

The uniqueness of the sermon lies in its function rather than its form but these are not always easily distinguished. There are genres such as story, poem, essay etc. Admittedly, the sermon may be treated as a genre, but only by forcing it. The genre of poetry is clearly different from the genre of essay, but is very difficult to distinguish the sermon as different as a literary genre *per se*.

The Uniqueness of the Homily

The recovery of homiletics hinges upon the rediscovery of the homily in its uniqueness. A sermon is not a lecture, it is not an essay, and it is not a counseling session—although to say this in no way depreciates these other ventures. In the midst of our uncertainty about what preaching should be, we would profit from a theological Gertrude Stein who would rise to declare, "A sermon is a sermon is a sermon." This means that if preaching is to be vital it must proceed from the center—preaching must be understood as *event*. The homily must then be understood in its uniqueness as the form of discourse designed to bring the word of God to expression in the concrete situation of the hearers.[7]

"Dynamic preaching" emerges from the uniqueness of the homily. Dynamic preaching, which understands the sermon as a series of forces interacting with one another, would thus take the place of "mechanistic" preaching which views the sermon as a construct of parts.[8]

The key to this approach is that its emphasis falls on what the sermon *does* rather than on what it is. We are indebted here, as elsewhere, to John Wesley, who stressed *verbs* in answer to the question "What is the best method of preaching?" Wesley answer, "To invite. To convince. To offer Christ. To build up, and do this in some measure in every sermon."[9] Preaching is understood not as the packaging of a product but as the evocation of an event.

A Definition of Homiletics

Homiletics is the creative and critical discipline that understands the homily as a type of discourse absolutely *sui generis* and in which the relationships consistent with the unique character of the homily are identified, developed, and expressed. Homiletics provides a framework in which

---

7. "Homily" and "sermon" will be used interchangeably throughout this work, but always presupposing this understanding.

8. This understanding of "dynamic" distinguishes the present work from existing references to "dynamic preaching" that use the term in a descriptive way.

9. From Question 54 of the Methodist *Discipline* of 1784.

true preaching can arise—a framework which serves the preacher both as a creative stimulus and as a critical apparatus.

Homiletics and the Theological Enterprise

Homiletics will play a large part in the total theological enterprise relating not only to rhetoric but the full range of theology. It was a fateful day when the venerable John A. Broadus asserted, in the work that was to become the standard in its field for generations, that homiletics was a branch of rhetoric.[10] Homiletics continues to redefine itself after this stroke which severed the head of preaching from theology and dropped it into the basket of rhetoric held by Aristotle.

Preaching theologically is our goal and that means more than preaching theology. Preaching theology means that theology is the subject matter of preaching, which it is. However, to preach theologically means that this subject matter of faith also informs why and how we preach. Theology of preaching therefore is not only reflection about preaching but theology itself.

The distinctions between homiletics and the other theological disciplines, while necessary as divisions of labor, are indefensible as stratifications into higher and lower statuses. At this point it is interesting to note that homiletics provides a link not only with the subjects traditionally concerned with ontology but also with those subjects traditionally concerned with communication. To clarify and strengthen these surely the teacher of homiletics must be ever sensitive to the wholeness of the theological task, for all the theological disciplines converge upon his specific area of concern.

That said, the field of homiletics, like that of the gospel, is the world. Homiletics must never be reduced to theological intramurals. Preaching must get out into the open air of intellectual discussion with "secular" disciplines. Such involvement will take many forms, some of them exciting, some of them dull, but all of them risky. Authentic language will be born only out of vital encounter with the world at its points of maximum stress, and the most torturous listening for the word.

---

10. Broadus, *On the Preparation and Delivery of Sermons*, 30–31.

The Vocabulary of Homiletics

It is the task of homiletics to understand the uniqueness of Christian preaching and to identify, develop, and express the modes which most adequately serve that uniqueness. For dynamic preaching, these modes are discovered in answering the question: What does the sermon *do*?

The answers to this question will provide the vocabulary for homiletics as a creative stimulus and critical apparatus. Following are dynamic understandings juxtaposed with mechanistic ones, in answer to the question: What does the sermon do?

1. The sermon deals primarily with a *concern* to be shared rather than with a topic to be explained. The sermon proceeds from the Bible as God's word to us and connects with the situation of the hearers; it does not arise from religion in general and address the universe.

2. The sermon moves fundamentally to *confirmation* from affirmation, rather than to evidence from axiom.

3. The sermon seeks *concretion* by bringing the meaning of the text to expression in the situation of the hearers, rather than abstraction by merely exhibiting the text against its own background.

4. The sermon seeks forms of *construction* and *communication* that are consistent with the message it intends to convey, not necessarily those which are most traditional, most readily available, or most "successful."

These elements are now established in the basic vocabulary of homiletics.

The question becomes, what must be added to meet the challenges of the twenty-first century? This is a guiding question in this exploration.

"How shall we *see* without a preacher?" is as crucial to the twenty-first century as "How shall we *hear* without a preacher?" was to the first. Ours is a visual age and we must communicate visually.

Although film and faith have been associated for years it is relatively recently that films have directly influenced homiletics and only very recently that they are influencing sermon preparation and presentation. The actual use of film making processes in preaching has been facilitated by digital technology that is widely available. This is still in its early stages and its development will be a major task for preachers in the twenty-first century.

We can trace some of this background to show that the affinity of motion pictures and preaching is not merely an expansion of technology. A fundamental connection between faith and film lies in the appeal of both to the imagination through visual and symbolic action.

Paul Scott Wilson urges preachers to become like moviemakers to engage our listeners. The biblical text comes alive as we picture a hillside through which Jesus and his disciples are walking as well as comment on the dialogue from the text.[11] Wilson develops this theme in various ways that are supported by his understanding of the larger poetics of preaching.

David Buttrick made a leap forward in his homiletic that included explicit use of film technique.[12] He has referred to my work as the Panasonic of preaching, just slightly ahead of its time. On that analogy, Buttrick is the Microsoft of Ministry, with Windows everywhere. In his *Homiletic* and other works, the window into filmmaking opens clearly into the future, and Buttrick's windows into a wide range of philosophical, theological and practical concerns will keep his work in the picture.

Richard A. Jensen's *Envisioning The Word* is a big step forward because it actually demonstrates the use of visual images in preaching with an illuminating discussion of the historical and theological background. The particular medium for this type of preaching is PowerPoint with its use of still photography and slide show. Like the earlier works I have mentioned this application is supported by Jensen's substantial studies in preaching especially regarding story.

Len Wilson and Jason Moore made a big move in *Digital Storytellers* in 2002. This is a valuable introduction to the use of visuals in worship including digital technology original motion pictures.

These works are important in their own right. They address people at significant stages of development. They also help us prepare for the production of sermons using motion pictures in a more fully visual worship setting and on the World Wide Web. They also reveal continuities and discontinuities. The next step is to develop a process.

---

11. Wilson, *Practice of Preaching*, 183.
12. Buttrick, *Homiletic*, 55–68.

The preaching of Augustine and Calvin represents the work of minds of great penetration that do not usually make unreasonable demands upon the reason. In our own time, the preaching and writing of C. S. Lewis is a storehouse of brilliant and effective reasoning. C. S. Lewis' life and work are like a castle with resources of such great value for Christian communicators that they must be studied and utilized as well as treasured. Lewis is the example par excellence of the communicator who masters a variety of forms to communicate his message: sermons, radio talks, essays, poetry, fiction, biography, not to mention the lectures and scholarly work of his profession. There is much to be learned from Lewis in each of their forms and all of them taken together. There are also critical adjustments to be made in translating his work into new idioms.

Jolyon P. Mitchell's *Visually Speaking* is highly recommended for several reasons. It shows why radio is a powerful medium worthy of contemporary use based on serious study of masters such as C. S. Lewis and others. It does this and more with a persuasive argument for a communications approach to preaching that opens possibilities for visual language in preaching in a variety of forms. *Visually Speaking* offers positive appreciation of the communication gifts of Lewis while warning against "Lewis idolatry." Lewis "scholarship" is important and improving as we see for example in Michael Ward's *Planet Narnia*.

Lewis's ability to communicate with children is shown in his enormously popular Narnia series. *Mere Christianity* is a prime example of his statement of the enduring content of the Christian faith. A collection of examples of his artistry in a variety of forms including sermons with his great "The Weight of Glory" is found in *The Essential C. S. Lewis*, edited by Lyle W. Dorsett. Among the professors who have examined his work critically and comprehensively are Armand Nicholi at Harvard University in *The Question of God: C. S. Lewis and Sigmund Freud Debate God, Love, Sex and the Meaning of Life*.

It is the film version of the *Chronicles of Narnia*, of course, that has catapulted Lewis into prominence and an audience rarely achieved by an academic let alone theologian. We are just beginning to see the enormous possibilities opening up from this in terms of further feature films of Lewis and his themes, opportunities to engage a variety of audiences in conversation, deepening of faith and stimulus of the imagination.

The combination of C. S. Lewis and Walt Disney is a spectacular combination of intellectual and film genius that hopefully will bear much fruit. We are sure to learn much from this collaboration that will inform us for the Century. One thing we already know however is that box office results while essential to big films do not adequately reflect the value of the art itself. The roaring lion of the MGM logo is not to be confused with the Aslan of C. S. Lewis. (Lewis' contribution and the attention being paid him are so huge that that we may miss the many humble entrances he offers to those who seek guidance.)

Ted Baehr plays a unique role in relating faith and film as executive and educator based at Movieguide. Aristotle being quoted to Neal Cavuto on Fox TV—how could this be possible? Yes, there was Ted Baehr enlightening the TV host on what makes a great film: the good, the true, and the beautiful. The same man who has been urging my theological colleagues and I to pay more attention to the media was there urging media leaders to pay more attention to theology.

So You Want o Be in Pictures by Ted Baehr is essential reading because it sums up the wisdom he has gathered from years of study and combines it with practical, down to earth guidance on every aspect of film making. F. Scott Fitzgerald lamented that while many people knew many things about movies no one grasped "the whole equation." This book by Ted Baehr and his ongoing activities do grasp that equation and shows how it illuminates art and theology and helps Christians communicate not only in filmmaking but also in other media. As Ted writes:

> Therefore, it is critical that people of faith and values become the best communicators through the mass media of entertainment. The New Testament uses five Greek words that we translate as "preaching" in English. The most common word is *kerysso*, which Jesus uses 63 percent of the time. It means to go into the marketplace to proclaim or herald the good news of the gospel. *So You Want to Be in Pictures?* intends to help you do just what Jesus commanded—herald his good news in movies and television.[13]

And so, what must be added to homiletics as it goes to meet the challenges of the twenty-first century? Recent developments lead us to this question with the "whole" and "parts" approach characteristic of hermeneutics. What are the parts of which Homiletics is the whole?

In the pages ahead we will be considering not only concern, connection, confirmation, construction, but also additional elements of context,

13. Baehr, *So You Want to Be in Pictures?*, xvii.

content, codes, conversations, concretions, and transformation. These are the parts of which homiletics is the whole when they are dynamically related in the eventfulness of preaching.

Thomas Troeger employs aquatic imagery for preaching in a way which complements Melville and Sweet. He tells how when he was a boy, his father built a small sailboat. Tom learned a lot from his father in that boat about sailing, and preaching. He learned how to move with the wind, and how to wait and watch when the wind was still, and they were becalmed in the center of the lake. Then when the wind came up, they were ready for an exhilarating lift.

Preaching is a lot like that. None of us can power it by ourselves, and there is no way that we can guarantee the presence of the Holy Spirit by our theory or method. But, as Troeger says, "like good sailors, we can use our skill to get ready for the wind, we can formulate strategies for preaching that open us and our congregations to the Spirit."[14]

As Jesus said to Simon and his crew, "Launch out into the Deep!"

And, as Paul might write to the Corinthians of the twenty-first century:

> Though I use the latest technology and theology
> And have not love,
> I become like a tinkling cell phone
> Or a beeping appliance.
>
> Love never fails.
> Whether there be predictions, they shall fail.
> Whether there be new programs and applications,
> They will be obsolete.
>
> Love takes time and is kind.
> Love enjoys the truth, not falsehood.
>
> When I was a child I played childish games
> But now I am an adult and it's time to grow up.
>
> Now we see on our screens, digitally,
> But then, face to face.
> Now we know in fragments,
> Then I shall know even as I am known, totally.
>
> There is theology, technology and love, but the greatest of these is love.

14. Troeger, *Ten Strategies for Preaching in a Multimedia Culture*, 7.

Two | Content and Concern

What's the Good News?

TWO PARISHIONERS TYPICALLY GREETED me on Sunday mornings and reminded me of my task. Alisdair was of the Old School, and he would meet me before the service to ask, "What's the Good News?" I would reply with a swift summary of my message and Alisdair would smile.

After the sermon another parishioner presented a different face, New School. Libby worked in the financial industry and was subject to all the ferocity of the killer city. Her characteristic word to me after the sermon was, "Get real with yourself!" Or to put it in her actual New Yorkese, "Get real widyaself!"

I learned to prepare myself for these two parishioners because I knew they spoke for all in my parish and every other. They want and need the message of Good News that deals with the real world in which they live and work. The dramatic growth of Christianity around the world testifies to the truth that in Jesus Christ, God meets us in our deepest needs and highest hopes. This is Good News. It means that in our moments of deepest despair we may hope and in our moments of greatest triumph we may be humble. The God who meets us in Jesus Christ makes this possible as Creator, Redeemer, and Transformer.[1]

This Good News is both shockingly simple and extremely complex. In its simple form it is expressed as "Jesus Christ"—Jesus is the Christ (the one you have been looking for is here). This simple claim becomes elaborated word by word until it fills books and then libraries, e-libraries, and communities as doctrine and commentary etc.

---

1. See my sermon on "Good News in Bad Times," in *On the Way after 9/11*.

The calling of the preacher is to communicate this Good News in ways that are simple enough to speak to children and complex enough to challenge adults. This would be impossible for humans alone but becomes possible with God. Evidence of this may be found in parishes all over the world as everyone who has preached a children's sermon with adults present can testify. I remember a preacher in a university church whose largest congregations were drawn on Boy Scout Sunday because that was the only time most people could understand him.

How Is the News Good?

The preacher is a theological Indiana Jones who interprets the sacred words that lead to the lost treasures and restore adventure and meaning to life. The simple Good News is so profound and has been developed with such complexity that it must be explored and interpreted anew in every generation from Neolithic to neon to network and beyond.

The Christian message in its most intense form is "Jesus Christ"—Jesus is the Christ. "Jesus Christ" is not a name like "John Doe" but a statement of faith like "I love you." It means when stated truly that this Jesus is the one we have been looking for all our lives and whom we now recognize. For the first-century Jew, "Christ" meant Messiah, the Anointed One. For the twenty-first-century seeker, Jesus is the one who loves us unconditionally, forgives us totally, accepts us where we are, and points us to where we are to go. When we follow him to live our lives with the passion and compassion with which he lived his we join an inclusive community of faith and service represented in the phrase "Kingdom of God" which is the Kingdom of God's people.

That we say Jesus is the Christ in the present tense testifies to the mysterious but real presence of the Promised One where two or three gather in his name and where God's word is preached and the sacraments celebrated. How this occurs is a mystery but in seeking to communicate it we find our meaning. The one whom we have been seeking is here and is calling for us. The mysterious but real presence of God where God's word is preached has confounded and comforted us from the Emmaus walk of Simon and Cleopas along the pathways of history to the electronic highway today.

This central claim was the message, the *kerygma*, of the early church. It was expressed in simple utterances and evolved into complex conversations, letters, Gospels, histories, and acts. Eventually these became creeds, summaries of the essentials of Christian faith. Then the creeds developed into doctrines, the doctrines into systems and institutions.

This complex system of belief is enshrined in the books and buildings of the church in its art and architecture and the bodies of those who worship there. These treasures may be lost on those present until the preacher like a theological Indiana Jones renders the meaning of the ancient inscriptions. The preacher interprets the claims of the faith as clues to the existence of the hearers and calls for their action. Like Philip, who finds an Ethiopian stranded by the side of the road, he or she interprets the directions and sends on him on his way. The preacher interprets the text so that the content of faith is seen to concern us, and to concern us ultimately, according to Paul Tillich.

The preacher is called to express the Christian message as a concern simple enough to be grasped by a child and complex enough to challenge a professor. The professor will want to explore the relationships of language and reality and how to transcend the subject/object dichotomy. Through exploring the professor can tell as well as the youth whether or not the message is coming through. If a preacher says literally "You are forgiven" in a way that says you are guilty, that is different from the expression that says goodbye to what I have been and hello to what I will become. In purely human terms this is impossible. Yet with God all things are possible, as we see in every generation from Jesus through Saint Augustine to C. S. Lewis and beyond. I believe that everyone who is reading these words has experienced such preaching at least once and would like to do so more often.

Yet what do we want to say? What is the Christian message for our media?

The answer to this question is simple enough to be stated in a sentence—the content of Christian preaching is the Word of God interpreted by the faith of the church in relation to contemporary people. *How* that is to be done is very complex. How this is done is very complex. Indeed it is one of the greatest challenges to faith. Søren Kierkegaard confessed in his journal that the greatest problem for him was not how to state the faith objectively but how to take faith up into his life. Few people have wrestled with this issue more vigorously than Kierkegaard and he did so with varying methods and varying success. Finally, though, Kierkegaard affirmed preaching as a means to this end by relating the abstract categories of theology to the basic issues of human existence. Thus the eternity of God is preached not as an ontological state but us an everlasting love. Kierkegaard's affirmation of preaching as communication in a direct form after an extraordinary exploration of various indirect means is worthy of further study. Certainly he raised the question of how the content of faith is to be taken up into life. Preaching is one way, when the content of faith is related to the existential concerns of the people.

The content of faith becomes the concern of the sermon when the intentionality of the text is related to the needs and hopes of the audience.

When this content is expressed in a particular homily, it becomes the concern of the sermon. By concern we mean that what is preached (content) is not simply information but transformation. The content of preaching is often referred to as if it were a thing. However "It" is experienced as if "it" is a person.

Concern

The heart of preaching is the sermon's primary offer of a concern to be shared rather than a topic to be explained. The *concern* is that which engages the attention of the preacher, forms the basic material of the sermon, and corresponds to what is usually known as the *subject* or *topic*.

Christians are convinced that the word of the living God as expressed in the Bible is the word that saves. When this saving word is creatively apprehended and shared by the preacher, he or she has the concern of his or her sermon. This word and this caring is that for which the exiles of earth yearn.

"Concern" here has affinities with Paul Tillich's usage of the same term in that it implies a dynamic relationship between persons and that that matters to them. The Society of Friends uses this word in a similar way. A Quaker arises in meeting to express a "concern" in his heart or a "concern" about a person or problem.

There is illumination to be found in the dictionary definition of the word that reminds us that "concern" is both a verb and a noun. As a verb, the word means "to relate to—be about; to have an influence on: *involve*." As a noun, the word means "something that relates or belongs to one: *affair*; matter for consideration." "Concern," as it relates to dynamic preaching, is a "verbal noun" that participates in both of the above definitions.

That is, it transcends the subject-object dichotomy by being at the same time a "thing" and an "event."

There are basically two ways in which we discover the concerns of others. One way to find out what concerns people is to ask them. Another is to use a diagnostic instrument with capacity for verification. The former may be called anecdotal and the later scientific.

The anecdotal reveals the stories by which we live. Some of them are told in private and the minister must address those concerns in ways that do not violate confidentiality. Many of these stories, however, are told openly in any service of worship at which they are invited. An opportunity for sharing the concerns of the people I regard as essential to worship. Of course this demands sensitivity and guidance from the leader of worship and with this will come revelations of the joys and sorrows literally from birth to death. In addition to brief announcements that often come in the form of requests for prayer, opportunities should be provided regularly for people to bear witness to what God is doing in their lives. Not all of these concerns are likely to be addressed in the sermon of the day, although some may, and certainly will be over time.

Essential as is this confessional resource, there are systematic ways to identify concerns that may or may not be evident in worship and to place them in a more verifiable context.

In Jesus Christ, God meets us in our deepest needs and highest hopes. This is the Good News! This Good News is addressed to the whole person across the whole range of human experience.

The Biblical Text in Its Intentionality: The Hermeneutical Hinge

The concern of the sermon is the biblical text in its *intentionality*. "Intentionality" derives from the Latin *intendere*, which means "to stretch." This etymology is helpful since there is a kind of plasticity in the Scriptures, which allows them to be expanded sensitively without fracture from the moment of their transposition into the written word to the moment of their transposition into the spoken word. The direction of the meaning of the text, as it enters and alters our life in the present, is its intentionality.

We have been speaking of *the* biblical text, but in what sense is this justified? At one level, of course, I am referring to the specific biblical passage or passages under discussion in a sermon. Yet if preaching is not to become a piecemeal exposition of scattered documents, one must have a view of the interrelatedness of the various passages of Scripture. At this level we discover that the question of the unity of the Bible continues to be exceedingly troublesome. About all that is widely agreed upon is the obvious fact that any answer must take into account the uniqueness and diversity of different texts as well as whatever they may have in common.

I propose that the understanding of *intentionality* provides a fruitful, albeit provisional, clue to the answer to this question. Simply put, it is that while the various texts of the Bible, Old and New Testament alike, present differing concerns, which reflect the uniqueness of their historical settings, one comprehensive concern permeates them all. Jesus Christ himself uttered it in answer to the question, "Master, which is the greatest commandment in the Law?" He replied, "Love the Lord your God with all your heart with all your soul, with all your mind." That is the greatest commandment. It comes first. The second is similar: "Love your neighbor as yourself." Everything in the Law and the prophets hangs on these two commandments (Matt 23:36–40; cf. Mark 12:28–34; Luke 10:25–28; 20:39–40).

The law and the prophets hang on the command to love God, neighbor, and self, and thus that command serves as the hermeneutical hinge. On this hinge, the law and the prophets swing into contemporary life. The concern for love permeates all the concerns of Scripture. Every text should be interpreted in such a way as to build up one's love of God, neighbor, and self, as Augustine observed in the first complete, formal study of homiletics, *On Christian Doctrine*.

This pushes us to a question, which is if anything even more vexing: What is the relation between the commandments to love and the Christ who utters it in the Gospels?

The importance of this question becomes clear when Paul Tillich confesses that his term "ultimate concern" is derived from the "great commandment" in Deuteronomy 6:5. Tillich is referring, of course, to the *faith* of the pious Jew in the God who commands, but even so, in our view, Tillich is mistaken to assign ultimacy to the Old Testament form of this commandment apart from its connection with Jesus of Nazareth. The old form is penultimate because in Jesus Christ there appear not only the commandment but, as Richard Kroner once phrased it, the commander. That is, we are not merely offered a new commandment, a new obligation, and a new work to perform. Rather we are given a new joy, a new hope, and a new source of power in the person of Jesus Christ.

The Gospel is fundamental. As 1 John 4:29 puts it, "We love, because he first loved us." Everything we do is but response to God's gracious action in Christ. This is what makes the good news *good*.

Following this point of view, one preaches *from* the Old Testament, but one does not preach the Old Testament. One preaches the New Testament in Jesus Christ and draws upon the Old Testament as a primary source of elucidation.

The Gospel means that the love, which is desirable for life, is available in Jesus Christ. The order *to* love is accompanied by God's offer *of* love. This love is never a cheap and easy sentiment. It takes the shape of justice and the form of the cross. Preaching it, as Paul well knew, is foolishness, but it is *God's* foolishness. And it is wiser than the wisdom of men.

If the commandment to love is the hermeneutical hinge of the Bible, the affirmation of God's love is the Door: "Thou shalt love the Lord thy God with all thy heart and soul and mind and strength and thy neighbor as thyself." Great as it is, this would be another Commandment were it not for the Commander God who loves us, in Creation, Incarnation, Redemption, and Transformation. As stated in Matthew, simply the content of biblical faith is, "You shall love the Lord your God and your neighbor as yourself because you are loved by God as Creator, Redeemer and Transformer." How then does the content of the Christian faith become the concern of a specific sermon?

The Attitude of the Preacher

We should also emphasize the importance of concern as an attitude of the preacher, which is implicit within the Scriptures to be interpreted. When the "word of the Lord" comes to the Old Testament prophet, it comes as a word that relates to the prophet personally. The prophet experiences the word—not as written on a tablet that he can toss off, but on his back as a burden that he cannot shake off. The prophet knows that his very existence is involved in the word he has been called to utter. As Jeremiah put it, the word burns as a fire within his bones. This sense of imprisoned fire is communicated in the written word of Holy Scripture, and nowhere more so than with the prophets of Israel.

The Given Biblical Text

The given in preaching is the biblical text. The preacher's donnée is the text, the verse or series of verses, which he or she intends to interpret in his sermon. On this basis the preacher prepares his or her sermon.

The text may be conferred on the preacher by a lectionary, or the preacher may choose it. Once it has been conferred or chosen, the preacher's fundamental obligation lies with the text. It may happen that some word or event in the life around him or her may offer the preacher insight into a text. Or an intuition apparently unprompted by Scripture may later be found to be consistent with a passage of Scripture. In such cases, the preacher must be sure to test his or her intuition against the norm of Scripture itself. In these cases, Scripture as the source of revelation, not as the origin of the creative process, is primary.

Failure to make this distinction between the source of revelation and the origins of a process has led, and still leads, to considerable misunderstanding about preaching and the Scriptures. Harry Emerson Fosdick is said to have disagreed with a faculty colleague who observed that, "You, Fosdick, take your texts from Broadway; but I take mine from the Bible." Fosdick could have countered that his colleague had suggested a dichotomy where it was not necessary. A sermon may begin with Broadway—an illustration from contemporary life—and still be thoroughly biblical, if Broadway is illuminated in this case by biblical light as well as by its own neon signs. Similarly, a "sermon idea" may be introduced into the preacher's mind by a word from a contemporary novel or by an event in current history. Its adequacy as material for the finished sermon, however, is to be tested by the illumination, which Scripture casts upon it.

The preacher should not approach the Bible with the expectation that it will have nothing to say to Broadway, any more than he or she should walk down Broadway expecting the Bible to have nothing to say to him. He or she will be moving in the right direction if he or she sees biblical meaning as the stage upon which Broadway stages are set. The authentic life for which Broadway yearns is the authentic life, which Jesus Christ confers.

The process by which we begin to understand a text or introduce a sermon may literally have its rise outside the Scriptures. The primacy of Scripture refers not to this process, but to its value as the source of revelation.

Such a distinction is also helpful with regard to what is known as "free text" preaching—the preacher chooses a text to preach toward a purpose that he or she had in mind. Such preaching is permissible when it does not allow the text to become a pretext (as the old adage goes) for the preacher's own opinions, but serves as the criterion for what is said. No preaching can be so free that it is no longer responsible to the biblical text, wherever that text may literally appear in the body of the sermon. Even if a biblical text does not appear in or with the sermon, the preacher is still responsible for evaluating his claim in the light of the biblical revelation, with reference to a specific passage or passages.

Establishing the text as the given with which the preacher will be occupied in his or her sermon is only the beginning. Let us say that we have our text for this coming Sunday. Now we must attempt to understand this text.

Understanding the Text and Understanding through the Text

Understanding the text is in many ways the most crucial aspect of preparing the sermon, since what the preacher asks here is precisely the question a member of his or her congregation will ask, "How may I understand this text so that I hear God speaking through it?" Understanding is the key to the hermeneutical interest. More broadly, hermeneutics is the study of the principles of interpretation—a study fundamental to Christian preaching because preaching takes its rise from a given text, which is to be interpreted.

A major development in recent studies may be summed up in the conclusion that the preacher seeks both to understand the text and understand *through* the text.

Visualizing the Text

Visualizing the text is the key to the shift from traditional to contemporary hermeneutics. Before, visualizing the text meant looking at the text metaphorically. Now visualizing the text means actually picturing the meaning of the text in ways that can be seen as in works of art. This involves "Visual hermeneutics" as described earlier.

It is important to acknowledge the visual as integral to the text itself. Of course, this element is crucial in communicating meaning as we shall see but it is no less important to understanding the text.

The visual and dramatic elements are inherent in the Bible itself. Jesus according to Mark asked, "Having eyes, do you not see? And having ears, do you not hear? And do you not remember?" (Mark 8:18, NKJV). Here Jesus was hearkening back to his Scriptures, and it is hard to exaggerate the emphasis Jesus place on the visual. The visual, of course, is a cue to the multisensory whole self-engagement with the message through the imagination. The legitimacy, and indeed the necessity, of visualizing the text are becoming more and more apparent in a visual culture. While this may have gotten out of hand in later allegorical interpretations of the Scriptures, we are now able to appreciate more fully the pioneering work of biblical scholars like Robert Funk,[2] Paul Minear,[3] and Austin Farrer,[4] who connected his New Testament studies with film studies. Richard Jensen demonstrates the value of this approach in relation to contemporary media. Doug Adams was likewise a pioneer in this field.

The Text and Its Context

Once the text has been chosen, the interpreter must attempt to enter into it, to understand it, we may say, on its own terms. The preacher's willingness to suspend his or her own interest at this point is not based on the assumption that he or she can step outside the text's claim on his or her life into some neutral zone. It is based precisely on the need to hear the text clearly so that his or her decision may be authentic. The moment of cold and sober analysis takes place within the context of one's personal commitment and for the sake of that commitment.

Wilhelm Dilthey once said that hermeneutics consisted of seeing the "I" in the "thou." Identification is essential if one is to interpret any historical phenomenon. There are those who claim that this is impossible and that the attempt to enter into the biblical text as a participant is futile. It would seem, on the contrary, that hermeneutics in the basic sense is

---

2. Funk, *Poetics of Biblical Narrative*. Two segments of this work are of special relevance here: the discussion of "Showing and Telling" in chap. 6, 133–62, and the discussion which relates the introduction to the film "Shane" and the Gospel of Mark in "Narrative Introductions" in chap. 9, 207–26.

3. Minear, *Images of the Church in the New Testament*.

4. Farrer, *A Rebirth of Images*.

not only possible but also necessary to life and is indeed carried out daily by everyone who is fully alive. Regularly we identify with our parents, with our ancestors, or with our heritage in order to gain understanding of them and of ourselves. Constantly we look at things from the viewpoint of others in order to understand them and communicate with them. The preacher's attempt to interpret the biblical text is merely a heightening of this activity.

The fundamental steps in attempting to put oneself in the other's place when approaching the biblical text are generally agreed upon:

1. *Consider the text* received in Greek or Hebrew in the light of textual variations, if any. The preacher should be able to consider the variations and reach a reasonable conclusion about the proper form of the text.

2. *Translate the text.* By this I mean here that the thought of the Greek or Hebrew is to be put into the basic language of the congregation. Pay attention to the key images as well as key words. At this point scholarship places immense aid at the service of the preacher—lexicons, grammars, dictionaries, concordances, commentaries, atlases, archeological source books and online services that link with visual and artistic resources.

3. *Relate the text* to its biblical context—immediate and total. Of what basic unit is it a part? If it is a parable, is it part of a series of parables? If so, how does it relate to the others in the series? Look at the text in terms of its larger biblical context. Here the advances in biblical theology in our time have great relevance and helpfulness.

4. *Visualize the text* (this emphasis is more recent). With the words and images from your study recreate a vision of the people in the passage acting out their drama. This may seem extraneous at first but it is becoming increasingly recognized by biblical scholars that much of the Bible is intrinsically and intentionally dramatic. This dimension will be a rich resource for composing and communicating the message.

These four steps will lead to the main meaning of the text in relation to its biblical context and contemporary horizon. The preacher, aided by the resources of modern scholarship, should by now have thought and felt his or her way into the situation of the biblical writer. This studying of the text may have its dry moments, but on the whole it is one of the most exciting and fruitful parts of sermon preparation. It has all the fascination of the detective seeking to reconstruct a crime, or of a novelist or filmmaker seeking creatively to enter the triumph and joy of others. And some of the most powerful homiletical clues will be uncovered at this point of study.

The Tradition of Faith

Understanding the text now leads us into one of the most essential and neglected areas of homiletical study, that of the faith of the church. A fully "historical" understanding of the text demands that we take into account not only the historical setting in which the Scriptures originated, but also the historical tradition by which these Scriptures have been handed down to us.

It is ludicrous, but not uncommon, to see preachers leaping—in the name of historical criticism—from the time of Christ to our own day as if historical tradition had no significance. Many reasons for this tendency may be found. The matter of exegesis and Christian tradition has been the subject of heated debate since the Reformation. Today, however, there is a growing consensus that the reformers have been misinterpreted, and that exegesis and historical and dogmatic studies must be carried out in dialogue with one another. This dialogue is necessary for the sake of preaching, if for no other reason.

It is no mere antiquarian interest that leads us to turn to Origen, Irenaeus, and Augustine, or to Luther, Calvin, and Bullinger for insight into a biblical text.[5] Rather, we may expect to find their words illuminating for a number of reasons. First, these men have been instrumental in shaping the church and culture of which we are a part, and—whether we recognize this or not—their thoughts and attitudes operate within our world today. Secondly, the genius of these men afforded them a grasp of scriptural meaning that sometimes eludes us, even with our improved methods of historical critical research. Thirdly, it is coming increasingly to be recognized in the Protestant tradition that the "Fathers" of the church in a broad sense have a right to exercise a certain authority—when this authority is placed in tension with the authorities of Scripture and of reason.

---

5. Note the two recent series: *Ancient Christian Commentary on Scripture* series, edited by Thomas C. Oden; and *The Church's Bible*, edited by Robert Louis Wilken.

Systematic Theology

The preacher's responsibility for understanding the text in terms of the faith of the church must be discharged in relation to the present as well as the past, in relation to the systematic theologian as well as the historian and historical theologian. The task of the preacher and that of the systematician are very close. Both are concerned with the bringing-to-speech of Christian faith in the present. Yet whereas the preacher is committed to voice the faith in the concrete situation of encounter, the systematician is called to reflect upon the faith in order to test its elements in relation to one another and the whole in relation to Jesus Christ and the contemporary world. Systematic theology thus offers the preacher a medium in which a particular text may be seen in a broader context of meaning.

Moreover, systematic theology affords a way of scrutinizing and relating the "middle terms" that arise between the text and the congregation. For example, when one preaches from a text dealing with "grace," it is illuminating to see how this particular text relates not only to the contemporary hearers but to the doctrine of grace in theologians like John Wesley, Paul Tillich and others. This sets the term in relation to other terms in the larger theological context. Systematic theology today is proving capable of shedding light in both directions.

Systematic theology also offers a discipline against which the preacher may measure his or her sermon of this Sunday with that of last Sunday, this season with that, this year with last. Systematic theology does not pretend to harmonize biblical passages that may be contradictory, but it may help the preacher see more clearly where the heart of a paradox lies and avoid unnecessary self-contradictions.

Here I am merely pointing out some of the major services provided the preacher by systematic theology; there are many more issues involved which demand a treatment of their own. It is clear that whatever contemporary preachers may *not* have learned from the systematicians, they *have* learned that often they are eloquent and homiletically quotable. Systematicians such as Karl Barth and Carl Michalson are writers of such virtuosity that their phrases move easily into sermons. This is good, but it is also dangerous. For the big question we have to ask of systematicians is not "Is it quotable?" but "Is it true?" That is, we expect the systematician to probe the meaning of Christian proclamation to its depths. We sadly misunderstand such a profound mind as Paul Tillich when we grudgingly complain of his three-volume systematics that "it won't preach." If Tillich is profound, we must not berate him because he is not simple. He is merely fulfilling his vocation as a systematic theologian. That the systematicians are often quotable is a bonus that ought to be collected only after the preacher has invested the time necessary to understand the context to which the quotable appears. By the same token, one luminous phrase may justify poring over a thick volume of dogmatics.

The preacher's conversation with the systematic theologians should enrich his or her understanding of the text in relation to the faith of the contemporary church and the modern mind.

The Text and Us

Seeing the text in relation to our lives and the lives of our contemporaries is part of the process of understanding the text. This contemporary reference contributes to our primary grasp of the text at the level of discovering the concern of the sermon; it is not something to be added to an already complete understanding of the text. We may achieve some of our most acute insights into the text when we see it in juxtaposition to our life and times. We must consider this matter as the preacher must—in relation to his or her congregation, in relation to contemporary art and science, and in relation to one's self.

My People

"What has this text to say to the particular congregation to whom I am preaching, for whom I as pastor have a unique and inescapable responsibility?" Whether or not this question is raised and answered may make the difference between a true sermon and a false one. A true sermon is an address to a particular people at a particular time in a particular place; it is not a general word to the universe.

The failure of preaching to "come home" to the congregation is a common and often justifiable complaint of laymen. Studies in pastoral care help immensely at this point. It was a turning point in the history of art when Renoir and other artists began painting portraits within landscapes. It is a turning point in preaching when the preacher begins to preach to faces, to particular persons and problems, seen against the landscape of their time and place.

Before he was to preach, a certain preacher would go into the empty sanctuary and sit in the pew of first this person and then that. As he sat in each person's place, he would try to picture the meaning of his text to him or her. What has this text to say to this man who is old and hard of hearing? To this young girl who is trying to decide whether to go to college or to work at home? To this young man who has felt a call to the ministry but is seriously involved with a girl of another faith? To this man who is a successful executive but who yearns for new life? Such questions as these, questions asked from within the existential situation, could throw light on corners of Scripture, which remain hidden from other analytical methods.

Myself

The question, "What does this text mean to me?" does not actually exist in a separate category. We have been asking it all along, and we never cease asking it. In a basic sense, it is the archetype of all human questions. We ask other questions, not only because of their inherent validity, but also to guard against narcissism, the absorption of the text into purely private meanings.

Nevertheless, there is a place not only for personal questions that I share with other persons, but also for purely personal ones, although they may never appear directly in the sermon. Thomas Wolfe wrote that all literature is autobiographical. Certainly all preaching is. The preacher should recognize this and, at a certain stage of sermon preparation, should let his or her imagination float freely over what may be of exclusively private interest to him or her. The result of this may appear not in *what* he or she says, but in *how* he or she says it—in the tone of conviction that issues from one who has felt a text applied to his or her life like a sharp sword or a healing balm.

My mother kept in her Bible small items that had special meaning for her. She was devout, and their presence folded between the pages of the Bible sanctified to her the memories of the persons and events they signified. The preacher would be wise to follow this example and write random notes in the margins of one of his or her Bibles. Every Christian should have a Bible that is fragrant with dried roses, brittle with the snapshots of children, colored with the faded print of newspaper notices, and charged with the electricity of notes from someone he or she loves.

This is the Bible in which you are most likely to find that the word of God is the very story of your life.

A further word is necessary at this point. There should be in sermons a real coming to grips with the relevance of the Gospel to the structures in which modern man and woman live. There should be a disclosure of man and woman's responsibility at such a level and in such terms as the hearers may respond to in their day-to-day lives. I will say more about this in the chapter on concretion.

The questions that we have considered are parts of the multi-layered structure that must be grasped if the text is to be understood. *Understanding*—this is the key word. To understand means literally to stand under a reality so that it throws light on our existence; it does not mean to "overcome" biblical material as if we were masters instead of servants. The goal of the preacher contemplating his or her text and the goal of the preacher confronting his or her congregation are the same—the hearing of the word of God; and there can be no true hearing without understanding.

The biblical text that is the given from which the preacher proceeds is not some objective *thing* back there in history to be grasped and then applied to modern life. Rather, the text is approached as a speech-event that discloses its meaning through its relationship to its context, to the faith, and to us.

This approach obviously militates against a formal homiletics that divides sermons into types such as "expository," "doctrinal," "life situation," and so on. It should be clear to anyone who ponders the matter that these titles apply not to discrete types of sermons but to motivations that should be present in every sermon. The harm done to both pulpit and pew by strict adherence to that formal homiletics is incalculable. It has spawned sermons on "social issues" that had no biblical frame of reverence and "expository" sermons that never got within speaking distance of modern life. It has tended to relegate historical and systematic theology to one type of sermon, called "doctrinal," instead of seeing the faith of the church as vitally involved in every sermon preached. There will be endless variety in preaching without such division into types. Every sermon should be expository, doctrinal, situational, and social at the same time, for these are the clues to understanding the text. These clues trace the line of meaning through the speech-event into our lives.

Content and Concern

When these questions have been asked and answered, we have the basic material for our sermon. Often the gist of the raw material can be listed on one page where one aspect can immediately be seen in relation to another, or the material may be kept on file cards. The preacher should allow his or her mind and imagination to play on this material until its force comes to reside in a single paragraph or sentence. Here, if he or she has done his or her work well, will be the concern for his sermon—the text in its intentionality as interpreted by the faith of the church.

The preacher is now ready to seek the connections and confirmations that will speak to Alisdair's question, "What's the Good News?" and Libby's insistence that it be real.

Three | Connection and Confirmation

TRYING TO REACH SOMEONE with cell phones is a frustrating but inevitable challenge. When we finally connect with the person and hear their voice the frustration turns to delight. Preaching is like this. Some sermons seem to get lost in dead zones while others come alive. The sermons that come alive connect and confirm.

Connection links that material to the concerns of the congregation and comes at the beginning of the sermon. Confirmation deals with how we support, authenticate, and engrain the material into the lives of the hearers and constitutes the body of the sermon. Continuity is important here for while connection tends to capture attention, confirmation must hold attention and carry it forward with substance.

How to reach the large number of African Americans moving in was a huge challenge to the existing largely Caucasian congregation and to me when I moved from my inner-city parish in Lowell, Massachusetts, to another in Wilmington, Delaware, after I completed my PhD program in Systematic Theology. The pastor's study in this Harrison Street Methodist Church parsonage was immediately next to the church building that housed our worship and program space. What a doctrine of ministry was enshrined in that architecture! The plus side was that the parsonage was conveniently linked to the church. The minus was the implication that the pastor could prepare his sermon in the study, step out on Sunday and preach it and return to work on the next sermon without interruption.

I knew that after a little time spent in that study I had to get out and into the streets to reach the people. I soon met a young African American boy named Eubie and I asked him what he liked to do in his free time. He liked to watch television. What had he seen recently what he liked? Eubie's face brightened when he talked about a movie he had just about these men who were trying to kill a big white whale. Moby Dick, I realized, and my smile must have brightened up as we talked about the meaning of the great white whale. That was a beginning of a continuing conversation with my neighbors with whom I connected thanks to Herman Melville, the John Huston film. This film is worth seeing again. Preachers especially will be impressed with the sermon preached by Father Mapple played by Orson Welles.[1]

We will return to the connective power of film but my emphasis here is on the necessity of connecting in preaching and ministry.

How connection is made and confirmed is of great importance in preaching and the subject is intensely discussed in homiletics today as it has been historically. There is a report in the New Testament itself that may mark the origin of this discussion. This is the discussion of the Great Commandment between Jesus and the lawyer which is referred to in Matthew 22:34–40; Mark 12:28–34; and Luke 10:25–28, with Luke extending into the Parable of the Good Samaritan. The report begins with the lawyer asking Jesus a question, appealing to him as "Teacher"—"Which is the great commandment?" Jesus answers, "You shall love the Lord your God with all your heart, and with all your soul and with all your mind. This is the first and great commandment. And a second is like it, you shall love your neighbor as yourself. On these two commandments hang all the law and the prophets." The lawyer agrees with Jesus.

At this point the connection has been made between the lawyers question and Jesus' answer. The information the lawyer requested has been supplied. Case closed we might declare. Not Jesus. The lawyer sought information and Jesus gave it to him, but Jesus seeks transformation and challenges the lawyer to do what he knows. When the lawyer balks at this and raises another question, what does Jesus do? He does not pressure the lawyer to act nor supply further argument to his appeal to the authority of the Scriptures. He tells a story, according to Luke, of the Good Samaritan. He then discusses the story with the lawyer, and when the latter shows that he gets it, Jesus invites him to act on his knowledge and live. The impact

---

1. Herman Melville who envisioned the pulpit as the prow of the world gives a detailed description of what he had in mind in the sermon of Father Mapple that occurs in chapter 8. This sermon on Jonah may be seen as a preview or synopsis of the novel as a whole. That we have on record what a great actor like Orson Welles can do with this is a treasure. The film was directed by John Huston, starred Gregory Peck as Captain Ahab and was produced by MGM, released in 1956. Welles was fascinated by "Moby Dick" and imagined how it might look on stage in "Moby Dick Rehearsed."

of this encounter on the followers of Jesus is clear, although the lawyer's response is not. The Gospel writers see this as essential to their story of Jesus and a demonstration of how His message is to be communicated.

Note the stress on "all." The commandment is to love "with all your heart and with all your soul and with all your mind." This appeals to the whole self while recognizing that the response comes in distinct but related ways. The Hebrews saw the self as a psychosomatic unity of body and soul while Greek thinkers isolated functions such as thinking and feeling. There has been tension if not conflict between these modalities from New Testament times to this. It was exacerbated by the enlightenment emphasis on "pure reason" and the adoption of academic forms of thought and expression as definitive for much homiletical theory. In this work we understand preaching to appeal to the whole person as an organic unity while recognizing identifiable functions for the purpose of communication. For example, appeals to reason differ from appeals to emotion although they are not totally separable or necessarily opposed.

That we are to love God and our neighbor as ourselves is the heart of Christian faith. Note that when the lawyer addressed his question about what was most important Jesus did not respond simply with the content. He knew that was already known to the clever lawyer. Jesus replied by emphasizing that this love was to be loved with all your heart, and all your soul and all your strength. With all! Then Jesus advised the lawyer to go and do what he already knew. The lawyer was seeking information. Jesus gave that to him but called transformation. This is dynamic preaching.

Dynamic preaching is concerned with transformation not only information. This means preaching to whole persons across the whole range of human experience.

Connection

What is the connection between the concern of the Bible and the concerns of the audience? When this connection is made, spiritual electricity is transmitted. The preacher is like a person making a conference call when a collective "Hello" signals that all the participants are on line. When this question is not answered, the sermon becomes like a phone gone dead.

Connection is more likely to occur when the preacher deliberately seeks it at the beginning of the sermon. This differs with the approach to preaching in which the sermon has a "subject" that has to be "introduced."

The introduction tends to become a preface to the material that is to be presented rather than an introduction of the audience to the text. Thus in its most obvious form the preacher begins, "Our subject or our text today is 'This.'" To understand "This," we must consider the background in which it is set. Such an approach may work in settings where people come expecting it but otherwise it only distances them from the message.

Dynamic preaching shares transformation as well as information and seeks connection with the congregation from the beginning by relating to the life concerns of the congregation. Addressing the concerns of the audience is as important as expressing the concerns of the Bible.

The Bible connects with the audience as food connects with the hungry. We need this nourishment. How the food is prepared and presented can make the difference between health and sickness. Therefore "connecting with the congregation" is of vital importance, as Robert Reid and Lucy Hogan spell out in their book with that title. In introducing their subject with a study of Martin Luther King Jr., they write: "preaching is an art of connecting with the congregation. It is acquired through the knowledge of principles, through understanding how master preachers before us—such as King—effected their persuasive ends, and finally through practice, practice, practice."[2] The first in developing this art, they claim, is to adopt a rhetorical stance.[3] They proceed to set forth a number of principles and practices that demonstrate the theoretical and practical values of his approach.

I am honored to be cited as an ally in this work. I especially appreciate the way in which the authors have perceived the positive thrust of what may have been the most controversial line in my original work: "It was a fateful day . . ." Some have missed my point and painted me as anti-rhetorical. The reader of the context of my widely quoted comment on Broadus will see that I am arguing for a rhetoric larger than that of Aristotle and for rhetoric seen as a branch of theology rather than the other way around. In distinguishing my approach from that of Broadus on these two essential grounds I further disagree that preaching is defined as argument. Rational argument is a valid and important tool in presenting the claims of faith, but preaching is more than rational argument and includes appeals to the imagination for example. In terms of mind-body

---

2. Hogan and Reid, *Connecting with the Congregation*, 9.
3. Ibid., 23.

studies, preaching appeals to the right-brain capacity for holism as well as the left-brain capacity for the linear.

The relationship of theology and rhetoric, of reason and argument and persuasion and related issues are much debated today and rightly so.

In the twenty-first century, preaching will engage in more serious dialogue with poetics and aesthetics and the imagination as it connects with a highly visual culture. This step forward into new media calls for a step back in understanding communications.

Mike Rhodes, an award-winning film director and producer, was asked recently where Hollywood's current interest in religion began. Rhodes paused, and then replied, "It began with Plato's cave and people watching the shadowy images on the wall." He went on to observe the ritual elements of going to the movies and how they were based on millennia of practice and observation. Thus the more we prepare for the future the more we will review the past and discover that we have more rather than less to learn from Plato and Aristotle as well as from Augustine.

Preachers have referred to movies in sermons for years but New Media have made it possible to show actual clips from the films in the service of worship and elsewhere. Mike Rhodes and Doug Adams pioneered in showing how film clips can introduce a sermon, appear in them, and aid discussion. Film connections and confirmations for the Scriptures through the church year and lectionary Cycles A, B, and C are presented in a fascinating way by Peter Malone and Rose Placate in their series, "Lights, Camera . . . Faith," which began in 2001.

Confirmation

Jonas Salk discovered a polio vaccine, then found that it was extremely difficult to persuade people to take it. Addressing the Royal Society of Health Congress in England, Salk warned that the responsibility that people do or do not take for their own welfare is one of the most important problems for a society. Every preacher is familiar with this problem. How does a biblical text move into the hearer's life in such a way that he becomes responsible for the world? Discovering the curative power of the biblical word is often easier than persuading people to "take it." *Confirmation* is of great importance, therefore, since it *is the process by which the meaning of the biblical text is strengthened, corroborated, and engrained in the lives of the hearers*. Confirmation tends to be the function of the main body of the sermon.

How confirmation works in dynamic preaching may be suggested by several analogies. First, confirmation is analogous to what certain psychologists call "insight." A moment comes when a situation is seen as a whole, and the viewer is given a clue as to how he is to act. The appropriateness of a type of behavior is confirmed.

The aesthetic sense has its own modes of confirmation. Beauty often confirms truth. At times we are, as Wordsworth put it, "Surprised by joy—impatient as the wind." Or, as John Keats put it in his classic "Ode to a Grecian Urn": "Beauty is truth, truth beauty." The moment of perception is the moment of awareness of reality.

Experience also confirms truth. Indeed, the truth that is "most true" for a person is the truth that his or her experience corroborates. "Sin" may be merely an obscure word until one sees how hideous life can become when twisted into self-absorption. And "grace" may be equally meaningless until someone whispers love in our ear. Then life puts its signature on our definitions. Experience confirms truth.

Insight, beauty, and experience—these provide some analogies to the way in which the meaning of a text is confirmed for us.

In dynamic preaching, confirmation takes over the work elsewhere assigned to *illustration*. Like illustration, confirmation is concerned with the illumination of the text. However, whereas illustration is typically regarded as the addition of stories, quotations, and poems to the material, confirmation means that the story or poem or whatever *is* the material. Confirmation does not embellish argument, it *is* the argument. The story itself must carry the weight of validating the intention of the text; one must not reduce the biblical text to abstractions that need to be enhanced by anecdotes. Confirmation *is* an integral part of the interpretation of the text. Moreover, whereas illustration often tends toward the sentimental and the pretty, confirmation is by definition yoked to the realities of responsibility. Ideally, the difference between illustration and confirmation is the difference between Norman Rockwell and Pablo Picasso.

Even more important, it is necessary to distinguish confirmation from "proof" as it is commonly understood in preaching. Confirmation does not seek to establish the correctness of a statement (as does a philosophical argument). Confirmation seeks to bring persons to the place where they may validate the claim of faith in their own lives; hence it calls for faith and obedience.

Reinhold Niebuhr, dealing with the matter of preaching in the modern era, writes that "The Christian Gospel as the final answer to the problems of both individual life and man's total history is not proved to be true by rational analysis. Its acceptance is an achievement of faith, being an apprehension of truth beyond the limits of reason."[4]

In spite of these and other well-documented insights from some of the profound thinkers of our day, many a temporary preacher labors under the delusion that it is his job to *prove* the truth of Christianity. He or she seems to try to "make a case," to "argue the point"—and too often he or she seems like a second-rate lawyer arguing a case in which he does not really believe. He or she is a kind of Perry Mason of the pulpit who differs from his or her television counterpart in that he or she *loses* all the time.

The sources of this betrayal of the genius of preaching are not hard to find. Generations of preachers have been tutored in homiletical theory that came near to idealizing the factual argument as the sermonic norm. For example, in 1929 a famous teacher wrote that "the quiet, earnest eloquence of facts is the only oratory which will succeed these days. Science has forced that."[5]

This statement was by no means eccentric for the homiletics of a day just past. The author was merely following the lines laid down by John A. Broadus in *On the Preparation and Delivery of Sermons*, which is regarded by many as a classic. Here, Broadus wrote:

> Argument, therefore, in the logical and at the same time popular sense of the term, forms a very large and very important element in the materials of preaching ... Preachers really have great use for argument.
>
> There are many gainsayers and doubters to be convinced, as regards both the truth of Christianity, and the truth of what we represent to be its teachings. There are many whom in both respects believe but whose religious affections and activity might be not a little quickened by *convincing and impressive proofs that these things are so.*[6]

---

4. Reinhold Niebuhr, *Faith and History*, 151.
5. Stidger, *Preaching Out of the Overflow*, 7.
6. Broadus, *On the Preparation and Delivery of Sermons*, 167–68; italics added.

The time has come for preachers to turn away from these seductive appeals. Faith can speak to alien forces only when it is unfolded from within its own unique meanings. These meanings are marked by the phrase, "according to the Scriptures," and by what we shall call kerygmatic reasoning.

The importance ascribed to the law and the prophets by the first Christian preachers is imbedded in the kerygma itself. The events heralded receive their significance because they occurred "according to the Scriptures." C. H. Dodd makes this clear. The church was committed "by the very terms of its *kerygma*, to a formidable task of biblical research, primarily for the purpose of clarifying its own understanding of the momentous events out of which it had emerged, and also for the purpose of making its Gospel intelligible to the outside public."[7] It is striking that Dodd regards the church's self-understanding through the Old Testament as more important than the apologetic value these Scriptures had in providing a point of contact with the dispersed Jews.

The kerygma was to be understood, *not* according to Greek philosophy, *nor* according to pagan naturalism, but *according to the Scriptures*. The Scriptures are themselves the record of revelation. The fundamental appeal of the kerygma is not from reason to agreement but from revelation to faith. There is thus an inescapably dogmatic element in preaching. The preacher shares something that has been offered him or her as a gift beyond his or her capacity to explain, and the preacher is vulnerable to the refusal of the message he or she shares.

The point of the authority of Scripture is dulled, however, when it expresses itself in the gesture of an upheld book with the rigid words, "The Bible says . . . ," or when it eventuates in proof-texting and the piling up of text upon text. The appeal to the authority of the Scriptures is actually the appeal to the living God who authors the Scriptures. The alternative to a biblical literalism is a biblical study employing a careful dialectical process.

The resources and standards for biblical studies grow and are refined from age to age. The preaching which shows the interrelatedness of biblical texts in terms of their mutual illumination is more to be desired than fervent appeals to the literal authority of the Scripture. Augustine did a brilliant job of this, utilizing the best scholarship of his day, which we

---

7. Dodd, *According to the Scriptures*, 11–12.

now see to be relatively primitive. A great deal of work needs to be done today on the basis of insights of recent and current biblical scholarship along the lines of Norman Gottwald and Walter Brueggemann. Gottwald pioneered a way of viewing the scripture in a more dynamic social context that illuminates both the Bible and our own situation. Brueggemann carries this forward in his own insightful and richly poetic writing.

Reason as the proper exercise of the intellect is as important to Bultmann and Niebuhr as it was to Broadus and Stidger. The former speak of "the limits of reason," not to dismiss reason, but to avoid unreasonable demands on it. Similarly, a theologian may set aside the reason of science (we might say, although Stidger was hardly correct in speaking of science in such a monolithic and uninspiring way) or the terms of syllogisms in order to penetrate to a deeper level of coherence. For such a theologian it is clear that the pulpit today is not suffering from too much rationality—far from it! Rather, too much preaching is burdened by a pseudo-rationality that sees the sermon as offering a lecture on the intellectual superiority of this or that aspect of Christian faith.

Reason is reasonable to the theologian when it is employed in the service of God. Two different statues symbolize the options. One is Rodin's famous "The Thinker." He sits curled in upon himself, his fist locked beneath his chin, his gaze completing the circle back into himself. The other statue is "The Prophet." He sits with the Bible in his hands, and his gaze is upward. Beneath and supporting him the sculptor has placed the hand of God. The preacher opts for the second representation as the proper exercise of thought. He or she finds it more reasonable to hold the Scriptures in his or her hand than forever to rest his or her chin. He or she finds it more reasonable to look upward than to contemplate his or her navel. He or she finds it more reasonable to believe that the hand of God supports him or her. Kerygmatic reasoning, which is characteristic of the New Testament, results from this latter posture.

The Greek word characteristically translated by the Authorized Version of 1611 as "reason" is *dialegomai*. This is the word used, for example, in the famous incident of Paul before Felix: "And as he [Paul] *reasoned* of righteousness, temperance, and judgment to come, Felix trembled, and answered, Go thy way for this time; when I have a convenient season, I will call for thee" (Acts 24:25 AV; italics added) It would be a mistake

Connection and Confirmation

to construe this "reasoning" as the construction of syllogisms, the statement of premises that lead to conclusions. Rather, *dialegomai* means to discuss, to converse, or simply to preach.[8] The parallel is more nearly with the dialectic of Socrates than with the logic of Aristotle, especially in that the face-to-face confrontation is essential to the unfolding of meaning in preaching.

The "reasoning" or dialectic in the preaching described by the New Testament and discussed here is kerygmatic reasoning has at least four salient characteristics. First, it tends to be reasoning *from the Scriptures* (see Acts 17:2), not from general first principles or axioms. Secondly, it tends to be reasoning *from the heart* (see Luke 5:22), from the vital center of human life, not from some abstract and isolated mental function that is not involved in the crucial issues of human existence. Thirdly, reason is employed to defend faith against wrong interpretations or false accusations (e.g., Acts 24:1–23). And fourthly, the reasoning tends to go beyond itself, to employ "proofs" merely as a means of attaining a foothold form which to make a leap.[9]

The history of preaching is marked by eras when the uniqueness of biblical reasoning was discerned with greater or lesser success. At one extreme was John Duns Scotus, who had full confidence that the human mind was capable of reaching certain knowledge. From this point of view, preaching was substantially a matter of supplying the evidence that would lead the mind to the proper conclusions.[10]

The question we must now seek to answer is—what modes of homiletical expression are most consistent with these bases for confirmation?

Story, poetry, reflection, drama, and visual art, and authentication by existence are among modes of confirmation that call for faith and obedience without seeking to remove the Christianity.

Parable

Robert W. Funk offers a clue to the primacy of parable for confirmation when he interprets Jesus' word to the lawyer who provoked the parable

---

8. Following Arndt and Gingrich, *A Greek-English Lexicon of the New Testament*, 185.

9. See Acts 17; Paul seemed to be doing well on Mars Hill until he spoke of the resurrection, which did not follow logically from what had been said before.

10. See Vier, *Evidence and Its Function*, esp. 118.

of the Good Samaritan to mean, "I ask you whether you understand—and your answer is your life."[11] In the same vein, Gerhard Ebeling has observed that "The parable is the form of the language of Jesus which corresponds to the incarnation."[12] The parable is the form in which understanding comes to life.

In the reading of a biblical story we are drawn into the drama; we become participants. Biblical stories share this captivating quality with the great myths and legends of other eras. Yet, even here, understanding the Bible demands the drawing of distinctions. Erich Auerbach, at the very beginning of his monumental work *Mimesis*, draws a contrast between the saga as employed by Homer and the saga as employed in the Old Testament.[13] Homer dwells on the externals of his characters and situations. He describes with extreme care the surface of environment and action. Everything is exposed to the light. Not so in the biblical saga of Abraham, for example. The narrator abruptly confronts us with the encounter between Abraham and God. There is little explanation of how they came to meet. Only as much environmental detail is given as is absolutely necessary to the story. An awesome presence seems to loom in the dark background, crying out to be interpreted. The dark presence crying out for interpretation, which Auerbach finds characteristic of the biblical saga, is perhaps the clue to a crucial distinctiveness of the biblical literature. He writes "Since so much in the story is dark and incomplete, and since the reader knows that God is a hidden God, his effort to interpret it constantly finds something new to feed upon."[14]

It is precisely the dark background of the biblical stories that are the sign of the authority of the Bible; they imply a second, concealed meaning associated with the hidden God. Auerbach's study is a brilliant example of the kind of parallels and distinctions that need to be drawn between the Bible and other literature. Moreover, it presents us with a profound

---

11. Funk, "How Do You Read?" 61. Cf. Funk's major work, *Language, Hermeneutic, and Word of God*.

12. Quoted in Funk, "The Old Testament in Parable," 251.

13. Erich Auerbach, *Mimesis*, 1–20. While I am in basic agreement with Auerbach's delineation of literary types, I must add that I am convinced that connections between the Bible and the life of our day are not obviated or reduced to "disembodied images" because of the change of environment and the rise of critical consciousness (cf. 12–13). The difference is that the claim for the "authority" of the Bible is not made *a priori*, but is allowed to reveal itself from within the Biblical stories in all its forcefulness.

14. Ibid., 12.

understanding of the way in which biblical stories may shock us into recognition of ourselves by sensitizing us to the "depths of time, fate and consciousness" of human being.

To the ancient appeal of tales the parables add some elements that angle sharply into contemporary life. Charles H. Dodd's *The Parables of the Kingdom* had a revolutionary effect on their interpretation. Dodd pointed out an alternative to the allegorical interpretation that had prevailed for centuries—the parables are not allegories but "the natural expression of a mind that sees truth in concrete picture rather than conceives it in abstractions."[15] Further, Dodd writes: "This leads us at once to the most important principle of interpretation. The typical parable, whether it be a single metaphor, or a more elaborate similitude, or a full-length story, presents one single point of comparison. The details are not intended to have independent significance. In an allegory, on the other hand, each detail is a separate metaphor, with a significance of its own."[16]

The preacher must learn, of course, not only to appreciate the biblical parables and to interpret them, but also to become a teller of parables. As Joseph Sittler put it, "*It is the task of preaching to enflesh these categories [of theology] with the living, episodic, and anecdotal concreteness of historical and present eventfulness.*"[17] Yet the misuse of the story is one of the sadder aspects of recent preaching. The story is such an alluring form that some preachers tend to become almost wholly anecdotal; story is told after story with hardly a pause for a point to sink in. Preachers scurry about for illustrations instead of devoting themselves to the less colorful task of exegesis. And, sometimes a strong story is expected to bear the weight of a weak sermon.

The response to the misuses of the story is not to rid the sermon of stories altogether in favor of a flavorless one-dimensional line of language. Rather, every preacher should make the mastery of parables a major enterprise. He or she should learn to select stories discriminately and to develop them carefully. He or she should collect resources of his or her own in notebooks or file cards and arrange them so they are accessible. He or she should learn to *tell* stories well. He or she should learn to harness the story to the intention of the text; it should pull the concern

---

15. Dodd, *Parables*, 5.
16. Ibid., 18–19.
17. Sittler, *Ecology of Faith*, 36; italics added.

of the sermon along, not ramble off by itself. He or she need not tell the congregation he or she is going to tell a story; he or she can just tell the story. He or she need not always make a point, then tell a story; he or she can tell a story and let the story make or be the point.

Above all, he or she should remember that the preacher is not a person who has to tell a story but a person who has a story to tell. Telling this story, he or she will claim the attention of adults and of children. They will be drawn into the drama and will be likely to extend it onto the stage of their daily lives.

Poetry

Preaching Poetically is this crucial element. That preaching is fundamentally an event to be experienced rather than an argument to be adopted has been basic. I suggested a series of alternatives drawn from biblical language to the essay as the form of the sermon—story, poetry, oratory, etc. It was the *story* that ascended to replace the *essay* with an overall liberating effect. The story will no doubt continue, but its limitations become more evident with use and overuse.

The poetic is emerging with new force in our pulpits, as well as our larger society. I mean poetic in the postmodern sense, of course, and not romantic verse—the intense language of symbol in which a word, image, or object is used for more than its factuality to portray the spiritual by the means of the material, or the invisible by the means of the visible. The symbol may take us directly to the reality it symbolizes, whereas, the narrative may take a route as roundabout as an argument.

Poetry and story have much in common, of course, and are not opposed to one another. However, there is a non-narrative element in poetry that remains largely unexplored in preaching today although richly developed by such past masters as John Donne and George Herbert.

That territory will become explored as the preacher seeks not only words but also images, visual images, and dramatic images that express the message in sermon and service through many different media.

Poetry can be prophetic. Notice that the great prophets are great poets, talking about Justice rolling down like water, and beating swords into ploughshares, and a New Heaven, and a New Earth. Isaiah, Jeremiah, Hosea, Amos, you can extend the list through the Old Testament and the New Testament and throughout history to Martin Luther King Jr., Vaclav

Havel, and others in our times like Mother Theresa, who only wanted to do something beautiful for God, to be a pencil in the hand of God. *In visions begin revolutions.*

> The most powerful political statement ever made
> was Jesus' poem:
> The Kingdom of Heaven is . . .
> within . . .
> you.
>
> That is why preaching
> begins in poetry
> and ends in politics.

It's exciting territory, a new frontier of the imagination for many. You get a sense of that in the poetry explosion from the popular Slam to the literary salons chronicled by Bill Moyers and others. You sense its potential for homiletics in the poetics of Thomas Troeger in sermon, hymn and lecture alike.

Visual Sermons

The visual element permeates the Bible although of course there were no cameras there to record the events. However, visual artists have long expressed this dimension. Now New Media makes it possible for preachers and local churches to develop visual preaching in a variety of forms.

Doug Adams wrote that visual imagery is the primary language of our day and draws together people of all ages, races, genders, and classes. People increasingly remember what they see more than what they hear. See Adams' *Eyes to See Wholeness: Visual Arts Informing Biblical and Theological Studies in Education and Worship through the Church Year.*

The importance of art to theological understanding as well as the enrichment of life is presented beautifully and persuasively by Jane Dillenberger in *Style and Content in Christian Art* and *The Religious Art of Andy Warhol.*

Church historian Margaret Miles helps make the case for using visual imagery, rather than just words, for sacramental purpose. She details in *Image as Insight* how during earlier centuries the visual arts made the church more inclusive, but verbal communication made the church more exclusive. Miles calls for a "Hermeneutics of Visual Images" that takes into account the similarities and distinctions in interpreting theological texts and religious images. Miles's journey of "understanding through the eyes" (Rudolf Arnheim) is demanding but promising.[18]

Today over 60 percent of our population, under age 60 and raised with television, remembers primarily by what is seen. Only 20 percent of the population, over age 60 and raised with radio, remembers primarily what is heard. (The remaining 20 percent remembers kinesthetically, that is, by doing). Churches having only verbal worship and preaching may as well use Latin, for the exclusively verbal mode no longer communicates with the vast majority of the population.

A woman at a dinner party was describing a drive in an Arabic country when her car was halted by a funeral procession. She was doing a pretty good job of describing the women dressed in black and their wild, wailing cry. Then she paused as if she had reached the limits of her descriptive powers and added, "It was just like a movie." To show the reality of her situation, she referred to film to connect us with and confirm her experience. It was as if with those words we could picture her more vividly as if she were in a scene from a film or television show. It happens all the time and is so characteristic of our times that we scarcely notice it—this tendency to verify reality by moving images on a screen. The dangers of this tendency must be addressed, but first notice its presence everywhere.

Moving pictures are the lingua franca of our time. Everyone speaks movies. The technical term for them is "time-based media," which includes film, video, digital art, etc. Bill Viola is a contemporary artist whose use of digital media is at the highest level. Viola's "The Greeting," based on a New Testament passage, was featured at the Venice Biennale and Grace Cathedral in San Francisco. *New Media in Late 20th Century Art* by Michael Rush places Viola's work in context. Peter Sellars also uses digital art in his internationally acclaimed staging of such works as the opera "El Nino," by John Adams.

"The language of cinema is universal," as we are reminded again and again in and out of movie theatres. There are many reasons for this that include cultural and commercial factors. But there are two aspects that have special relevance for preaching.

One aspect is that film has a language that communicates across cultural boundaries. For example, linguists and anthropologists had studied the Pirahã tribe in South America for years in an effort to grasp their lan-

---

18. See Miles, *Image as Insight*, esp. 27–39.

guage without success. Then they experienced a breakthrough that may upend the entire field of linguistics and force new directions, according to John Colapinto in *The New Yorker*.[19]

Dan Everett and his wife Keren had gone to the tribe as an evangelical missionaries whose mission was to translate the Bible into the Pirahã tongue. Their marriage dissolved; but Keren continued her mission of Bible translation while Dan stayed to pursue his academic interest in what represents "the minimum foundation necessary for human language." Keren has found that the key to the Pirahã language is the tribes singing or "prosody."

The breakthrough for Dan came after many years of research on an evening when he invited the Pirahã to come to his house to watch a movie, Peter Jackson's remake of "King Kong." The Pirahã responded to the film immediately, enthusiastically and knowingly. Colapinto writes, "If Fitch's (Everett's colleague) experiments were inconclusive on the subject of whether Chomsky's universal grammar applied to the Pirahã, Jackson's movie left no question about the universality of Hollywood film grammar."

The phrase "the universality of Hollywood film grammar" is the point. But what makes this account so significant is how it documents the point with reference to Christian mission, Bible translation, cultural anthropology, linguistics, and film in a narrative form "to be continued."

Further, in analyzing how that transaction had taken place, the scholars were led to an advanced understanding of language itself. Something happens in film that has important implications for all communication especially preaching which is concerned with event.

Another aspect is that the visual and dramatic elements are inherent in the Bible. New media do not introduce them, but they can help communicate them. Ironically, it is the oral tradition that carries the visual for the telling of the stories and the recitation of the poetry and the sharing of the wisdom were often performed in public in the marketplace as popular entertainment in their time.

Before exploring how this shapes the construction and composition of sermons, consider Jesus Christ floating over the city of Rome in the form of a statue being waved at by beauties sunbathing on rooftops but unnoticed by street-bound citizens is an image from Federico Fellini's

---

19. "The Interpreter." Dan Everett addresses the issues also online: www.theedge.com.

film *La Dolce Vita*, which captures the missed connection between Christ and culture. Such a Christ is like Robert Lowell's prisoner, "Hanging like an oasis in the air of lost connections," which characterized much of the twentieth century. The danger of film images is precisely that they become mere images rather than symbols in which we participate. The image becomes a substitute for our lived reality.

The twenty-first century presented an alternative vision early on in the "Passion of the Christ" film by Mel Gibson. This was no statue floating above the "sweet life" but a person dropped to earth, bloodied and crushed in our midst and before our eyes. The enormous reception of that film shows the force of the moving image to connect with people today and confirm the power of the biblical story.

It is easy to criticize that film and its maker, but what are we to do with that Jesus Christ and his cross?

Four | Construction and Composition

Tʜᴀᴛ ᴛʜᴇ ᴠᴀʀɪᴇᴛʏ ᴏꜰ biblical forms influences the shape as well as the content of sermons is now widely accepted. Here we will look at the basis for this point of view, sharpen it, review the most widely used forms and focus on three not widely used but that hold great promise for the twenty-first century: Poetic preaching, Visual Sermons, especially short films, and Brief Forms.

Frank Lloyd Wright inspired a revolution in architecture when he claimed that a building should be built, not *on* the ground, but *from* the ground. A revolution in homiletical style is inspired by a similar claim— the sermon should not be *on* a text but *from* a text. That is, the sermon should not be slapped onto a text, extraneous and superfluous to it, but should rather grow from the text organically. The sermon is not a superstructure attached to a text, but a vital extension that sets the text in motion in the lives of the hearers. The form of the sermon would then follow this function.

Developing the structure that best expresses the message is the task of construction and composition. Construction is the term traditionally applied to this and it has a splendid tradition based on craft. Composition is useful in bringing with it the creative dimension associated with the arts and this dimension is especially useful in the visual and aural aspects. The tools of composing a picture or music expand the possibilities of preaching. See, for example, Michael Graves, *The Sermon as Symphony*.

Biblical form criticism made it clear that the fundamental forms of the communication of the Gospel did follow the function of address— confrontation with the claims of the kingdom and the call to new life. The brief proclamatory utterance, the parable, the dialogue, and so on were the forms which arose naturally from the preacher's intention to direct men to a new life orientation.

Similarly, sermon composition means to the contemporary preacher the process of discovering and employing the communication structures that best convey the meaning of the biblical text to the hearers so that they are moved to respond to it. Referring to "communication" rather than to merely "verbal" strictures marks a significant shift from earlier homiletics that dealt almost exclusively with words whereas today communication involves visual and other nonverbal aspects. The renewal of preaching in the twenty-first century requires development in this area for two fundamental reasons. One obvious reason is that our audience today communicates visually as well as verbally. Equally important but no as often recognized is that there are visual elements inherent in the Bible that were obscured by the rise of the printing press but are being recovered by new media.

The value of employing concepts and methods of photography and filmmaking are set forth convincingly by David Buttrick, Thomas H. Troeger, Paul Scott Wilson, and others. Jensen's book, *Envisioning the Word: The Use of Visual Images in Preaching*, is especially valuable because of his statement of the understanding of faith and art that under gird his work and his earlier understanding of story and narrative preaching.

The next step that I advocate here is to add motion pictures to the forms of sermon composition and communication employed by the preacher. The most accessible of these forms is the short film or viral video which typically runs from 30 seconds to a minute and may be used in church, on the world wide web and broadcast television, the latter in the form of PBA (Public Broadcast Announcement, better known as a commercial). Even this short form would not be available to most churches were it not for the advent of high quality, low cost digital media. However, if you can make a good thirty- second film you will learn the basics of what you need to know to make a longer film, including one of feature length.

Before going into further detail on method it is important to view the overall context of composition and construction since there are continuities and discontinuities between verbal and visual structures and both must be taken into account. Neither I nor the others whose work I cite are arguing for a replacement of the verbal by the visual but rather an expansion. This expansion implies not only the use but the criticism of film and new media.

The verbal structures to be considered are primarily oral rather than literary. Biblical scholarship has clearly shown that the oral traditions that give rise to literary form are not accidental but reflect the origin of religious language in the calm or frenzied utterance of the human voice. "Faith," as Paul said, "comes by hearing." Amos N. Wilder comments on Paul's rhetoric, highlighting its oral character: "The very nature of the Gospel imposes upon him ways of expression that suggest dramatic immediacy: devices and rhythms of the speaker rather than the writer; . . . challenges not so much to understand the written words but to listen and behold; queries, exclamations and oaths."[1] Thus the oral emphasis is inherent within the Gospel itself.

Christian preaching proceeds from concern to concretion; therefore the moment of living presentation is crucial. Whether the truth of faith will connect with the hearer and reach concretion in his experience hinges on whether the preacher communicates the intention of his or her text with the resources God has given to him.

The strength of the statement of thematic with propositions derived from the text lies in the concern of this method for communicative structures. This method seeks not merely to reiterate the biblical text but to convey what it means in terms of the lives of the hearers, to spell out the implications of the text in a form that the hearers can appropriate. The weakness of this method is that the propositional form is not characteristic of most of the biblical material itself, and something of biblical meaning is often lost in the transference into this form. Furthermore, there may be observed a tendency to drift away from the biblical message into statements of "universal" application that are related to the biblical text only slightly, if at all.

It is important to understand this form of preaching because while it is not essentially biblical it is essential to the development of preaching and virtually defined homiletics until fairly recently. Indeed, "sermon" referred to a statement based on a biblical text or topic that consisted of an introduction, a series of propositions or points with illustrative material, and a conclusion, often poetic, followed by a prayer.

---

1. Wilder, *Language of the Gospel*, 22–23.

This form is shaped more by the teaching function than New Testament. Augustine defines it in the first great study of homiletics, *On Christian Doctrine* that refines biblical study and enhances that with insights from classical Greek philosophy. Augustine has much more to contribute to our understanding of preaching than his oft-cited *Confessions*, as I demonstrated in "Augustine's Theology of Preaching." A recent biography that updates this is James J. O'Donnell's *Augustine: A New Biography*. Augustine learns from rhetoric but denies that preaching is rhetoric because preaching transcends it. The preacher is a teacher, but preaching reshapes teaching as Christian revelation reshapes Greek philosophy. The Christian preacher examines life as thoroughly as Socrates, sees transcendence no less than Plato, and follows the argument as strenuously as Aristotle. The Christian appeal to authority is more rather than less than pagan sources. For example, Plotinus referred to God as the love lovelier than all the loves of earth, beauty more beautiful than all the beauties of earth, etc. The Christian preacher is more than a teacher but never less. He or she is the "Doctor" for whom the "Doctrine" is the subject.

That said, while the form of the lecture (spoken discourse) stating an argument and illustrating it is not characteristic of biblical language, it is not completely foreign to it. For example, Paul's sermon on Mars Hill has many of these characteristics but that story may owe more to the author of Acts than to Paul. However, the Sermon on the Mount, the New Testament epistles, the sayings of Jesus, Proverbs and the Wisdom literature all contribute to the teaching function of Christian preaching.

Study Augustine's actual preaching and we discover that Augustine was a master of the sermon that met the requirements of the classroom and the public square, the town as well as the gown. Augustine's sermon on the Fall of Rome in 410 is both a classic and a contemporary. It is an oration, a statement intended to be spoken, and heard, with lessons to be learned, and a lecture. It is also an essay—a personal exploration of a theme which expresses a point of view and appeals not only to reason but imagination, shared experience and other sources. The essay has many of the aspects of a letter, but as a sermon form, it is intended to be spoken in public as well as read in private.

Mastering argument, Augustine realized that faith moved beyond sheer logic. Logic can clarify what is known, but how do we move from the known to the unknown? Augustine answered, "We tell a story. We appeal to the imagination and weave that into the sermon."

Construction and Composition

Augustine has much more to teach us. He mastered the sermon in the context of liturgy in an historic way, but he did not stop there. He extended his preaching in less formal settings where he literally engaged in conversation with those who had questions and problems in an early example of the dialogue sermon. He carried on an active correspondence with many. He wrote for those outside the church. His Confessions is a classic of literature, as well as faith, and many believe it created a new genre of writing. Activities like these are traditional now but they were new media then.

With all the strengths then of the sermon that is a lecture arguing the case for Christianity, what is the problem? The problem is that preaching is much more than this and suffers when so narrowed. Yet that narrowing happened in the earlier part of the twentieth century, began to be challenged outright in the 1960's and continues to be challenged today.

Behind the strengths and weaknesses of these traditional homiletical methods lies a problem that keeps us from an either-or situation—the genuine tension between the structure of the biblical text and the structure of the communicative word. If merely the biblical text communicated itself, preaching would not be called for. If the communicative word were all that was called for, the biblical text would not be necessary. The sermon is the communicative word with, from, and through the biblical text. Therefore, there is an inherent tension in the preacher's task. It is not merely some generalized uneasiness; it is a tension that arises every time the preacher preaches—a tension between the structure of the text and the structure of communication.

Preaching is therefore a creative process, because the tension cannot be relieved by simple laws and rules. There is no single answer to the question of the relationship between these two types of structure. Every sermon is an adventure. Still, there are basic clues that may aid the preacher in his discovery. The first is that *in coming to understand the text and in planning the sermon, the preacher must take the literary form of the text into account.* The second is that *the preacher must seek the sermonic form that best shares the intention and mood manifest in and underlying the text.* The third is that New Media offer contemporary ways to express graphically the visual elements inherent in the literary forms and the oral traditions behind them.

Types of Sermon Structure

Story

The story and the narrative form was the biblical structure for preaching proposed in the 1960's that moved to the center of discussion. John McClure writes that narrative preaching is that in which "some agent of narrative exerts a controlling influence on the sermon":[2] "Although these debates are likely to continue, it is clear that the study of the relationship between narrative and preaching leads directly to the center of contemporary homiletics. The garden of narrative has been tremendously fertile for homiletics over the past thirty years, and homileticians will likely continue to gather fruit there in the years to come"[3]

An exceptionally effective use of this type of sermon construction is found in the preaching of Frederick Buechner. His sermon "The Magnificent Defeat" is simply magnificent.[4]

Narrative preaching is so widely discussed now that we shall turn to poetic preaching which is not.

Poetic Preaching

Walter Brueggemann calls for poetic preaching in *Finally Comes the Poet*:

> By poetry, I do not mean rhyme, rhythm, or meter, but language that moves... that jumps at the right moment that breaks open old worlds with surprise, abrasion, and pace. Poetic speech is the only proclamation worth doing in a situation of reductionism, the only proclamation, I submit, that is worthy of the name preaching. Such preaching is not moral instruction or problem solving or doctrinal clarification. It is not good advice, nor romantic caressing, nor is it a soothing good humor.
>
> It is, rather, the ready, steady, surprising proposal that the real world in which God invites us to live is not the one made available by the rulers of this age. The preacher has an awesome opportunity to offer an evangelical world: an existence shaped by the news of the Gospel.[5]

---

2. McClure, *Preaching Words*, 93.
3. Ibid.
4. Buechner, "Magnificent Defeat," in *Magnificent Defeat*.
5. Bruggemann, *Finally Comes the Poet*, 3.

Construction and Composition

Poetry and religion go together. In moments of religious experience when the soul is at one with the eternal harmony of God its utterances often become rhythmic and burst into song; common prose is not adequate to express its joy or its longing, in rhythmic rise and cadence flow forth praise and prayer revealing the deepest feelings and desires.[6]

The sermon is theology in images. Albert Camus wrote in his notebooks, "The novel is philosophy in images." Similarly, the sermon is theology in images that evoke, convince, persuade and move us. "Poetry and religion go together," said Bewer.

However, there are problems that arise in the consideration of poetry and preaching. The bad reputation of poetry among some preachers is most likely rooted in certain homiletical usages, such as quoting a sentimental poem in lieu of solid thought, rather than in the nature of poetry itself, since poetry is akin to preaching. Preaching in which the natural affinity with poetry is adequately expressed may be called "poetic preaching." It is distinguished by the following characteristics:

1. Poetic preaching is preaching which is sensitive to the rhythms of speech, although its lines are not likely to be rhymed or made to follow the same metrical pattern.

2. Poetic preaching is preaching which is concrete in its imagery, not vague or flowery.

3. Poetic preaching is preaching which is structured according to its function, but which is not therefore formless.

4. Poetic preaching is preaching which is aware of the connotations of words, of nuances of speech, and of the value of hints and suggestions beyond explicit statements.

5. Poetic preaching is preaching which does not so much state a thesis as create an effect.[7]

Nearly all-great preaching is poetic preaching in one or more of these aspects. In our own time, there are conspicuous examples of highly effective poetic preaching.

---

6. Bewer, *Literature of the Old Testament*, 340.

7. I am indebted to Maurice Bowra for this language. He says of Paul Valery that his poems do not so much state a thesis as to make an effect. See Bowra's *Heritage of Symbolism*.

Thomas H. Troeger demonstrates the poetry of preaching in a remarkably illuminating and instructive way. He is a poet in the formal sense showing mastery of form in his hymns. In his sermons, lectures and prose as well he exhibits an eye for imagery and an ear for the rhythm of language. His unique contribution is in the ways he connects these traditional gifts with New Media as shown in his work, *Ten Strategies for Preaching in a Multimedia Culture*. Troeger offers practical suggestions although this is not a "how to" book. Much is gained in understanding the Scriptures as Troeger demonstrates writing the sermon as a movie script, creating a parable and playing with images and other strategies.

Ernesto Cardenal is a major poet who is an ordained priest. I asked him how he related his poetry and his preaching. He replied, "My poetry is my preaching, and my preaching is my poetry." His work supports his claim and offers much from which we can learn. See Cardenal's *The Psalms of Struggle and Liberation*.

Alan Jones shows how poetry can be interwoven in preaching in a style at once elegant and conversational. This Dean of Grace Cathedral in San Francisco talks with you rather than at you in sermons that combine biblical insight, solid argument, keen observation, and a wide range of references from the arts and current events. He extends his preaching and the ministry of the Cathedral through a pioneering Internet mission, superb performing and visual arts programs. Alan Jones is a poet and this is a key I believe to his effectiveness as a communicator. In fact, one of the first times I heard him in public he was reading a poem in a program at the Museum of Modern Art in San Francisco.

Preachers have much to discover and delight in with contemporary poets. Poetry readings that may be found all over the country are a storehouse of wit, wisdom and eloquence. They should be familiar territory for the preacher along with the poetry chapbooks and print and online versions. I find contemporary poets to be a rich storehouse of spiritual no less than secular insight. James Joyce once called for an art that could hear God in a cry from the street. That cry and many other shouts are heard in the poetry of David Madgalene as we hear in his "God the Cruiser":

> Up and down the avenues of Broadway
> ...in a city of no shame and no knowledge
> of guilt but no denial of pain.

> On Broadway, along with the beaters
> and the beaten, the downfallen and
> those who rise up in a moment of
> glory and flash.[8]

Visual Sermons

Preparing a visual sermon is like preparing a traditional sermon with your eyes opened more widely as the field of vision enlarges. We study the biblical text for content, but also with an eye on the visual element. For example, as Simon and Cleopas take the Emmaus way, what does that look and sound like? This involves the visual hermeneutic so important to the artist like Rembrandt and so neglected by traditional preaching.

In the twenty-first century, the visual element will play a larger part not only in understanding the text but in composing and communicating the sermon.

The relevance of film method to preaching has been convincingly set forth. The next step is to apply those methods to the actual filming of the sermon, i.e. composing and communicating the sermon in visual forms. Likewise as one seeks the concerns, connections, confirmations and concretions of the sermon one imagines how they appear visually. Thus when you come to the composition of the sermon you have a rich store of visual material.

The tools of composition include computer programs that integrate word and image and prepare them for presentation on screen. Among the most popular of these programs are PowerPoint and iMovie.

Short Film

The short film clip, often only 30 seconds in length, is a key that opens many doors. It is familiar in the typical TV commercial and online, a staple of both establishment and emerging venues. It is used in Public Service Announcements (PSA) as in the United Methodist Church's "Open Doors, Open Hearts" series, as well as in PSA's by other denominations and local churches. Its brief form encourages use on church websites where it can be quickly downloaded. It can be produced inexpensively with digital camera and computer in the iMovie format from Apple or similar programs for PC's. It is also the basic building block of the larger

---

8. Madgalene, "God the Cruiser," 110–12.

film of documentary or even feature length. Learn how to make a short film and you will know the basics of making a feature length film. The beginner may find this hard to imagine but already there are local churches that have gone from the short film to creating and producing the feature film distributed by a major company and seen by millions. "Facing the Giants" is one such film.

The short film is the entry point to film making for many students and indeed faculty at the Graduate Theological Union where I teach. Some of these students come to seminary with backgrounds in film studies but most learn the basics quickly when motivated to do so. Our Communications Project at the GTU has been prolific enough to generate many works good enough to be celebrated in a festival, which we in fact do every year in our New Way Media Festival. These works are used in worship and education programs. Often students go on to develop short films into longer ones.

An outstanding example is the aforementioned Yerko Ban, who began such a project in one of our classes and then expanded it into the film, *The Vricino Brothers,* which earned him recognition from a famous institution in Stockholm, Sweden.

Ken Wales is a Hollywood filmmaker associated with the acclaimed film, *Amazing Grace*. I asked him what he thought theological schools should be teaching future ministers about filmmaking. He replied, "Storytelling! Storytelling! Storytelling!" Storytelling is indeed the key—Digital storytelling as it is called with the advent of this technology that has made it possible for every church to be in production.

This is, of course, one of the major thrusts of the homiletic that has championed the story and narrative forms of preaching as alternatives to lecture forms. In both preaching and film story refers both to a specific tale and to the structure of the tale. Thus preachers learn to tell the story of Noah and the Ark for example and to tell it within a story that has its own structure as an interaction between the preacher and congregation.

Examples of a Visual Sermon

I teach New Media including visual preaching including film making by what I call "mutual mentoring." This approach presupposes that both teacher and student bring essentials to the process rather than one being the maestro to the other protégé. The teacher does lead by creating the situation in which he or she can interact creatively with the student. For example, I tend to know more about theology than my students who tend to more about technology. By collaborating we are more likely to develop a deep theology with high technology to best communicate.

A prototype for a short visual sermon is "Wigs Off!" This is a 30-second PSA that I have used to announce the New Way Media Festival and also shown to the class as a demonstration.

My son, daughter-in-law and I had made a visit to the Asian Museum in downtown San Francisco. Leaving the museum, we happened upon a commercial being shot for Dove Shampoo in the Civic Center. Seizing the opportunity, Judy filmed the commercial being filmed, and I made some brief remarks, which were also filmed.

Normally, one storyboards the presentation before the film is shot, as a guide. In this case, we shot the rough footage first and then entered the film into iMovie. iMovie has a feature where one can break the film into different clips, thereby creating a de facto storyboard and that's what we did.

"Where Are the Leaders of Faith?" was a short film, available in both 5-minute and 15-minute versions, which we made showing the religious response to 9/11 which was not being covered by the major media. This film was an official selection at the Berkeley Film and Video Festival.

"Opening the Bible" was a 30-minute film of a class worship presentation that was also an official selection at the Berkeley Festival.

We have made other short movies, as well. While there are different thresholds to achieve in terms of presenting your films, and these are rising higher all the time, still a film need not be "Hollywood quality" to serve a function in your classroom, church or on your Public Access station or elsewhere.

Storytelling

One of the basic tools for film story telling is the storyboard. Further, as mentioned earlier, iMovie and similar movie-making programs incorporate the storyboard into their design. I highly recommend Ted Baehr›s book, *So You Want to Be in Pictures*, and *Storyboarding 101* by James O. Fraoli.

Students

"Sounds like you want to put the *Mysterium Tremendum* on the Internet!" These words from an examiner came in response to a seminary student's statement of vision for his ministry expressed in a committee of which I was a member. They were loaded with skepticism and scorn. The student who had prepared for seminary with a degree in film studies met the challenge head on and affirmed that indeed it was his vision of ministry to communicate the mysterious and tremendous Holy using New Media. In that encounter a gap between students entering seminary early in the twenty-first century and those charged with educating them opened wide—teachers quoting Latin and students speaking electronics.

That gap is not as wide now as it was then and much credit must be given to the students who saw something in advance of many of their teachers and kept driving toward their vision. I have been fortunate in knowing some of them. Each of them is a distinctive individual who contributes to a growing common understanding.

Thirty Seconds to Raise the Dead: Brief Forms

That the preacher has twenty minutes to raise the dead has been famously quoted for years but today the preacher has thirty seconds for that is the period of time anyone can count on the attention of the audience. With that, the speaker will win or lose more time.

This is the sound bite in which the news must be encapsulated. At first it sounds ridiculous. How can anything be meaningfully expressed in such a short time? Often it is truly absurd, as when a TV host said to a guest, "What can we do to avert another 9/11 disaster? You have thirty seconds to answer."

Absurd as it may sound the preacher today must master this genre. Not only does it stand alone as in the case of Bulletin online or a PSA for a church or but also it can be decisive in the context of a sermon. The concern of the sermon should connect in just this form.

It helps to understand why the sound bite exists and how it functions since it is obviously limited and easy to criticize. Newscasters discovered that due to the short attention span of viewers and the limits of time and space news was best reported in increments beginning with the minimal thirty seconds. A news item itself required a minute and a half so a "bite" of that taking thirty seconds announced at the beginning of a news segment could alert the viewer to what was coming next. If that sound bite captured the attention of the viewer they would stay tuned for more of the story. Of course, major stories required more time and in extreme cases there would be continuous coverage and eventually documentaries, etc.

The effective sound bite must have enough substance to stand on its own but attract attention for further development. Supplying the context to the sound bite is crucial.

The good news is that this requirement of media helps us recover one of the most basic forms of the Bible: the Saying. These are brief statements also known as proverbs or sayings. They are basic to the Old and New Testaments and essential to Jesus. In Hebrew the base is *davar*, a rich word that may be translated "word" and "thing." In Greek, the base is *logos* or *logoi*, word or words. The Greek also uses the verb *legō* in this connection which may enlighten those who grew up with toy blocks with this name and learned how to link things together with them.

The importance of these functional sound bites are everywhere found in Jesus and the first preaching about him, i.e., "Jesus Christ is Lord" in the context of kerygma and creed, which are also relatively brief forms.

Proverbs and "saying" sound bites are a staple of religious, literary and oral traditions as in wisdom sayings, maxims, aphorisms, and epigrams. As an example of the language dynamic going on the saying or soundbite, I refer to my late friend Henny Youngman, the King of the One-Liners. His most famous one-liner, still widely used, is, "Take my wife . . . please." Of course it's all in the timing. However, notice the dynamic. Take my wife (a straightforward statement, straight line) . . . Please (a leap to another level: punch). Response: Laughter. A complete theory of language is implicit in this dynamic. I got to know Henny in New York and once told him that the Bible was full of one-liners. Henny was dubious, but the next time I saw him he had done some Bible study and agreed with me.

I found in the parish that one of the best uses of this form is the Affirmation. An Affirmation here refers to a line from a sermon that can be used in prayer and meditation.

I show how this works in my book *The Power that Heals* and give examples in *On the Way After 9/11*. State what you want to say as and clearly and briefly as you can in a paragraph. Write it out or talk it through. Eliminate every unnecessary word. Restate the essence in one sentence. Try different arrangements of the words until the most stirring and memorable phrase results. Study past masters of the forms.

Five | Communication

ONE SUNDAY WHEN I was a student pastor, I noticed a woman in the congregation who was thoughtfully taking notes as I preached. I was flattered to think that I was saying something so valuable she wanted to take it home. After the service, I discovered that she had left the note in the hymnal rack. It said, "2 loaves bread, 1 pound butter, 1 quart milk . . ." What I thought were my immortal words were her grocery list. The question is, how do we get the bread and wine of the Gospel on the same table with the bread and butter of our audience?

The answer is to be found in the communications revolution that is sweeping through churches around the world leaving some on fire and others burned out. Preachers on fire without being burned out grasp communication as Performance, Production, and Process. We begin with Performance since it involves the presentation of the sermon to the live audience physically present in the same space with the preacher. Then we look at production that involves presentation through media to those not present in the same physical space. Then we consider the communications process that underlies these activities and connects them to the mission of the church leading to transformation.

Performance

"Performance" is the word now widely used to describe the actual presentation of the sermon to the live audience, as Jana Childers demonstrates in her book, *Performing the Word: Preaching as Theatre*. For many years in America, but not necessarily in other times and places, this was confined to the "delivery" of the prepared sermon, and when this approach began to appear in homiletics in the twentieth century, there were objections that preachers where not actors and preaching is not performance, and so on. Indeed, there are important distinctions between the actor and the preacher. The preacher, unlike the actor, is not pretending to be someone saying things they may or may not believe.

The shift from delivery to performance, however, has roots in philosophical and theological understandings and relates to language as performance as well as dramatic method. So much is to be gained from this approach that "performance" and "audience" are terms increasingly being used along with "delivery" and "congregation."[1]

Preaching from the Heart

Preaching is one person speaking from their heart to the hearts of others about the heart of God. The prayer of Psalm 19:14 expresses the heart of preaching. The triad of communication embraces God, the congregation and the preacher in the event of preaching. The sermon is first an offering to God and then to the people. I have offered this prayer aloud before preaching throughout my ministry and it has evolved into the form stated at the beginning of this work, "Let the words of my mouth and the images of our media, and the meditations of our hearts, be acceptable in your sight, O God, our strength and our redeemer."

People have a desperate need to hear someone speaking from their heart about things that really matter. We see this in churches, just as Robert Bly does in poetry readings. If what is being said does not matter to the preacher, it is not going to matter to anyone else. And it matters to the preacher. It matters to the preacher whether people live or die. It matters whether he or she is telling the truth. It matters whether people get the Good News and not just the bad news. It matters that the minister cares in a world that often does not.

A minister was standing at an intersection waiting for the light to change when a man with dark glasses and a cane started across the street. "Wait," said the minister, and pulled him back as a car approached. "People will run right over you," said the man with dark glasses, "nobody cares." I care," said the minister. When the light changed he walked the man across the intersection toward the school for the blind. A minister can help a blind person across the street, even when they may not be able to restore

---

1. Richard Ward uses similar language independently in his instructive *Speaking from the Heart*.

sight to the blind; and in that word and deed of caring, they preach the Good News.

That compassion carries over into the church where the preacher seeks to help people across the careless streets of life because it matters.

To the Hearts of Others

"Everybody has a hungry heart," sings Bruce Springsteen. The heart hungers for love, identity, meaning, and more in millions of appetites. These hungers can be fed by faith through preaching and sacrament, as James Wallace convincingly shows us in his book, *Preaching to the Hungers of the Heart*.

A heart surgeon talks directly with the person on whom he will be operating just before the procedure. He or she tells them that in the moments ahead he or she will be holding their heart in his or her hands and will do everything he or she can to make it strong. The preacher is like that surgeon in a way which is less literal but equally profound. The preacher, like the surgeon, dares to take the heart of the hearers into their hands knowing that words cut like a scalpel and heal like medicine.

About the Heart of God

The preacher cares because God cares. We love because God first loves us. God opens the divine heart to us in Jesus Christ to show us how much we are loved, even unto death on the cross. God gives God's Word to us in the Bible to reveal that this love speaks through Creation and Transformation as well as Incarnation and Redemption. The need to love and to be loved is the deepest human need. That need is met in the love of God of which we sing: "Love divine all loves excelling, Joy of Heaven to earth come down."

No one need feel that anguish in the ultimate relationship of life. We look at the Cross that is God's love letter to the world and we know for sure, God loves me. This empowers me to love God in return and my neighbor as myself.

To address these needs, I must *speak of the heart of God*. Speaking from our hearts to the hearts of others becomes preaching when it is of the heart of God. We are not simply talking, but talking about things that matter most. What matters is our relationship with God. This is what Paul Tillich called our ultimate concern. We are concerned about our health, our families, our finances, our community, and many other things; but our ultimate concern is whether or not we're reunited with the One who can energize us for all other concerns.

The good news is that God is concerned about us. In Jesus Christ, God meets us in our deepest hurts and highest hopes and brings us new life. The heart of God is at the heart of Christian preaching.

For years it was assumed that the Gospel was an object that could be pointed to in words, and indeed we had just these words in the Bible. If we would preach from passages of the Bible, then we would preach the Gospel. This assumption underlies much of our thinking about the use of the Bible in worship via the lectionary, as well as preaching specifically. There is an industry that has grown up around the production of worship and homiletical aids organized around this notion. This assumption is questioned today from many sides. We must take the questions seriously.

God is the answer to the question implied in our lives. This good news comes to us from God who opens the divine heart to us in creation, redemption, and the support of life itself. The heart of God is at the heart of Christian preaching. Preaching at the party is speaking from the heart to the hearts of others of the heart of God.

Let us sum up our answer to the question. How are we to preach at God's Party? The sermon is the event in which we speak from our hearts to the hearts of others of the heart of God. Preaching is the process that includes this presentation along with the preparation that precedes it and the follow-up that comes after.

Three aspects of performance are basic to preaching: General Appearance, Bodily Movement, and Vocal Quality.

General Appearance

The general appearance of the preacher should be appropriate to the occasion and to the preacher himself or herself. For those in liturgical traditions where correct garb is prescribed for each occasion, this pretty much takes care of itself. One of the advantages of this tradition is that robes can cover a multitude of fashion sins.

More and more preachers are taking that risk and casting aside their clerical robes in favor of clothing that identifies them more closely with the congregation. Wearing a suit instead of a robe, however, does not in itself improve communication anymore than wearing a Hawaiian shirt makes you an Hawaiian. What wearing a Hawaiian shirt in the chancel can do is help connect with other people in the congregation who are wearing them, or wish they were.

What one wears in the chancel is far more of a choice now, and this is a mixed blessing. On the positive side, making these choices conscious helps one re-think the relationship between clergy and laity, the audience or lifestyle to which they wish most to appeal. On the other hand, being overly conscious of these matters can draw attention to the preacher and away from the message. It is best to think of general appearance as simply one aspect of communication in expressing oneself and relating to the congregation.

Body Movement

Where the speaker stands and how he or she moves involves "body language" as eloquent as words. The pulpit literally defined the place of preaching until the 1960's when a few preachers began moving away from it to get closer to the congregation by moving among them and interacting with them. In my own case, I began to do this when I experienced a positive reaction on the part of the people which overcame the alienation I felt from them looking down on them from the lofty height of the chancel. I remember the Sunday I made that step out of the pulpit and into the congregation. I was preaching on the incarnation and was frustrated because my voice was reaching the congregation but the message was not. The great truth of the incarnation was turned back by the fourth wall between preacher and congregation, no less formidable than the fourth wall presupposed by the proscenium arch of the theatre. How to break through that wall?

Well, Jesus Christ was divine. God. Second person of the Trinity. He held a place of privilege similar to that of the preacher, clothed in official garb, occupying a place high above others, protected by the armor of the pulpit. Yet what if the privileged one were to leave that place and move among the people. Here I did simply that—walked down from the pulpit, past the communion rail onto the same level with the congregation. That got their attention. What I had done in a small way, God had done in a great way. I continued, and took off my robe and rolled up my sleeves to suggest what God had done in Jesus Christ. No on went to sleep during that sermon and I could tell from the conversations later that we had moved to a new level of understanding.

Preaching after that did not always have such developed dramatic action, but where and when we use body movement and gesture to emphasize the message we are more likely to communicate. Joe Webb advances this discussion by showing that freedom to move while preaching without depending on the pulpit or notes is essential to preaching in the contemporary service.

Production

The preacher today and tomorrow will become more and more familiar with production values and processes for projecting the sermon in the worship setting and beyond by video and internet. The preacher himself or herself may have little aptitude for technology and assign production matters to a staff member or more likely team, but the more one does understand and appreciate what is involved , the more likely they are to communicate effectively.

It is no accident that one of the most effective preachers of the early twenty-first century learned his art as the television producer of his father's ministry—Joel Osteen. In his New York Times bestseller *Living Your Best Life Now*, Joel reveals that he believed his calling was not to be a preacher. Rather, he believed hat he was called to work as a producer of his father's television ministry. This for him was a Holy calling and he devoted his life to it. Osteen considered every aspect of the service to be televised to find the most effective ways to communicate the message his father was to deliver. In particular, Osteen devoted great care to the design of the pulpit itself so that it could be a means of communication and not a barrier. Then just as Osteen had completed that crucial task, his father died. He felt that no one could fill that gap, but someone had to preach. In that situation, Joel Osteen felt the call to preach, and from the pulpit he had lovingly and brilliantly crafted for his father, his ministry was launched. The rest, as they say, is history. All that he had learned about television production elevated that ministry to a new high. Of course more than production is necessary. Osteen has found ways to help people live their best lives now, and they respond.

Critics complain that Osteen's message is the "Prosperity Gospel" and even heretical to some. They say that his message is too optimistic. Osteen's appeal, however, is biblically based, inclusive, and he does not shy away from the problem of suffering.

One of the benefits of widely-known ministries like that of Osteen and Warren is that they bring to the surface many critical issues. The responsibility of the audience is to sort out the issues rather than to blindly agree or disagree with the communicator or the critic.

Indeed, in time, Osteen will no doubt expand his message. Anyone who can look into a TV camera and say, "Friend" to a million people and make each one feel he is talking to them is doing something right. We can't imitate him, and we shouldn't try; but we can learn from Osteen, especially in the area of preaching and television production.

Rick Warren and Saddleback Church illustrate another way of producing television for worship. Their emphasis is not on broadcast but on closed-circuit TV. At Saddleback, there may be several different venues where people are gathering to worship in distinctively different styles simultaneously. At the time for the sermon, the message is delivered live from one of those congregations to the others. This makes for a clear and consistent message from the pastor with attention to the differing needs and lifestyles of the congregation.

Media ministries are growing rapidly all around the world but there is no one model for them. I believe this is a good thing, for it encourages every pastor and congregation to develop his or her own authentic ministry without mimicking another. A helpful guide is *Media Ministry Made Easy* by Tim Eason.

Process

When I was a pastor in New York City, another woman parishioner made some notes for me that were much more constructive than the woman who left behind her grocery list in my student parish. Dr. Esther Thorson was then a professor doing research at Rockefeller University. In conversation I asked her about her work, and she sketched an outline for me of a series of small rectangles connected by lines with the possibility of different kinds of connections or disconnections. She then described a variation of the communications process that had been developed at Rockefeller by Harold Lasswell, and had become a foundation of communications theory and practice. Her research was in a contemporary application of that theory. I found it to be helpful in what I was trying to do in preaching and pastor work.

Dr. Thorson developed her work to become a distinguished leader in strategic communications and education with a special interest in New Media.[2] She is currently a teacher and administrator at the School of Journalism at the University of Missouri at Columbia.

Recently I discovered a stunning application of that theory: It is a basis of web design and indeed of the Internet itself. Lasswell's model of communication provided a core around which a science was developed. His model divided the process into parts that can be summed up like this:

> Who?
> Says what?
> To whom?
> In what channel?
> With what effect?

Lasswell's original formulation is one of those strokes of genius that seem obvious once stated, but before he had developed it, it was not so simple. Indeed the subject had been examined by Plato and Aristotle. It was Lasswell's use of his theory, however, that provided a vocabulary with which to phrase the questions and to process them. His primary assignment dealt with espionage in World War II, but applications have proliferated in business, politics, technology and elsewhere. Today we find evidence in every time we turn on the television or go online. The standard design of every effective website must answer those questions posed by Lasswell.

Norbert Weiner provided a major addition to Lasswell's theory in developing cybernetics, dealing with the interacting of people and computers. Wiener found that there was a need for interaction in the process and so was born the feedback function.

The immediate application of this approach to the preacher is its usefulness in designing the church website and using the Internet. Much more is at stake. Every preacher has a communications theory, whether they know it or not. So does every congregation. The better the preacher and congregation come to know this process, and work constructively with it, the better their communications will be in preaching, worship, mission and every aspect of church and community life.

---

2 See the cutting edge book edited by Thorson and Schumann, *Internet Advertising*.

The preacher and the church can be more than passive users of an instrument designed originally for military and commercial use. They can be critics of it and transformers. This process or a variation of it underlies most of the communications taking place today. Given what appears to be a scientifically tested theory, why are there so many communications failures today at every level, from the home to the United Nations?

A large part of the answer to this question lies in a flaw in the theory. As it stands it works well for selling a product, like shampoo or cars. Yet it falls short because it lacks a vital element. It lacks the elements of meaning and purpose and values.

These elements are familiar to preachers through their study of hermeneutics in theology. Traditional hermeneutics is the study of the interpretation of the Bible while in the New Hermeneutic it becomes also the interpreting of life in the light of the Bible. The hermeneutical circle is the term that refers to the interaction between the interpreter and the text he or she attempts to bring to understanding. This arises in the work of Friederich Schleiermacher, a hospital chaplain in Berlin in the nineteenth century. As Schleiermacher attempted to communicate the understanding of Scripture, he discovered that his audience already had some understanding of the material. He called that a "preunderstanding," and realized that it had to be taken into account. The interaction between the interpreter and the text is the beginning of a circle that widens to include those to whom the interpretation is addressed.

What is missing in the commercial model of communication is found in the field of hermeneutics in philosophical and theological studies. The missing link is understanding, which involves meaning and purpose. The question of *why* must be dealt with. When this happens, we do not merely add a word but change the whole process. The question of purpose pervades the whole process adding depth and giving direction.

Hermeneutics is the interpretation of the Bible. For many years it has dealt with the question of what the text meant. A New Hermeneutic has turned attention to what the text means that has far reaching consequences. Schleiermacher found that in interpreting the Bible to his congregation he needed to involve the pre-understanding of the people in the understanding of the text. That is, people do not read or hear the Bible simply as it was originally written. They already have understanding of the words being used and situations to which they refer. This needs to be taken up into the process of understanding the text and this interaction between the interpreter and the interpreted Schleiermacher called "the hermeneutical circle."

This approach initiated by Schleiermacher was welcomed by philosophers who developed it extensively and made it a hallmark of modern philosophy: Dilthey, Heidegger, Gadamer, et al.[3]

Schleiermacher developed it as a corrective to prevailing communications theories of his day that sought to "explain" texts rationally but missed their deeper meanings. The usefulness of the hermeneutical circle comes into play today because it offers a corrective to prevailing communication models. The hermeneutical circle introduces subjects that deepen and widen communications including meaning and purpose.

I have found a variation of Lasswell's approach to be increasingly helpful in preaching, teaching and personal life, a variation that involves a process including feedback and clarification.

One of the major problems in preaching is the assumption on the part of the preacher that the congregation is hearing what he or she is saying. Likewise many parishioners think that if they say something to the pastor, the pastor gets it. The pastor may indeed get it, but it may not be what the parishioner intended. The Roundtable approach advocated by John McClure and others has values, one of which is just such a process including feedback.

Today the questions of the Medium or Media used in communications must be included in the process.

The understanding of communications that has emerged from studies of these technological subjects applied in ministry may be stated:

> *Who* says *what* to *whom* by what *media* with what *effect* with what *feedback*.

The hermeneutical question arises out of the study of the meaning of life from the questions of Socrates and the Greek tradition and the Hebrew Bible and New Testament. Here we deal with the central issues of life that concern not only what car we buy but where we go in it.

The hermeneutical circle needs to be employed as well as the communications cycle to express the fullness of faith and meet the range of human needs. The hermeneutical circle to the relation of the interpreter and the interpreted in relating parts and whole at the core of under-

---

3. For more on Heidegger see the Commentary. Especially helpful in this discussion is Hoy, *Critical Circle*.

standing. The circle implies interaction between the interpreter and the interpreted that implies a circle of persons paying attention to a common concern and surrounding it with meaning. Thus the hermeneutical circle refers both to an intersection of the interpreter and the interpreted and the interaction between the interpreters.

This subject deserves continuing study. However, its relevance here is to add the question of purpose to the communications process thus deepening the whole process.

The communications process for preaching may be stated thus:

Who says *what* to *whom* by what *media* with what *effect* with what *feedback* with what *meaning* and to what *purpose*?

These questions can be stated in the form of their subject matter as follows:

- Messenger
- Message
- Audience
- Media
- Effect
- Feedback
- Meaning
- Purpose

The hermeneutical circle is essential to understanding dynamic theology and preaching because it identifies and combines concerns without which the subjects tend to become static. Principal among these concerns is that of the spiritual and transcendent which are not present in many theories of communication.

However, the hermeneutical circle is not a panacea for communication ills and is subject to problems of its own. It can easily become a closed circle. Therefore, the communication cycle is also important for theology and preaching.

The strength of the communications cycle is that it incorporates concerns for feedback and outcomes without which communication becomes static. It offers data based on empirical evidence that is helpful in evaluating communication.

The communications cycle also has problems because it tends to become object-and-sales-oriented, and narrowly commercial.

Dynamic preaching calls on both the hermeneutical circle and the communications cycle.

This is done short term by synthesizing the two approaches in a practical way and long term by research and analysis. This makes available the richness both of the hermeneutical and communications resources in the communicating of the Gospel—Who says what to whom by what media with what effect with what feedback with what meaning and to what purpose.

To the claim that this superimposes weighty theoretical framework on the preacher, I reply that in fact all of these concerns are implicit in the process of preaching itself and that raising them to consciousness and putting them on the table enables us to better employ them.

To the claim that this approach solves all problems in preaching, I reply that it does not. Both the hermeneutical circle and the communications cycle have the virtue of inclusiveness and movement but tend to circle back upon themselves and close. The communication evident in the Bible moves beyond this. There is a shift in which the communication is lifted to a new level. The day of Pentecost is but one conspicuous example of this. When they were all with one accord in one place, the Holy Spirit descended tongues of flame.

On the one hand, this transformation was a gift of God unmerited by any theoretical or practical worthiness on the part of those who received it. On the other hand, had not the community been hard at work, and had not Peter mastered his subject, the gift would not have been received as it was.

The element of the gift of the Holy Spirit, without which preaching is dumb show, cannot be reduced to a hermeneutical method of communications technology. Yet the methods and technology can be placed in readiness and in service of the sacred. People like David, and Peter, and Paul, believed that when they placed their best upon the altar, God would bring the fire. Their faith was fulfilled, but the task is not finished.

The preacher and teacher of preaching today are called to clarify on that task. This means drawing on both hermeneutical circle and communications cycle. When these are visited by the Holy Spirit, the circles become a spiral lifting us to a new level, transforming us no less than our age.

Communication

In asking, what does this mean?, the approach I find most useful is one among others. Whatever school of communications one follows the preacher must understand that it is a process that includes feedback, or they will be forever like that young preacher whose immortal words were lost in the parishioner's grocery list. Sometimes communication is most effective where it is least self-conscious.

I had heard much about Prof. Thomas Boomershine as an advocate of electronics in the church. So when he came to speak at the Fourth Fosdick Convocation on Preaching and Worship at the Riverside Church in New York City, I went with hope, mixed with skepticism.

My skepticism emerged first. I came upon the man who was obviously the leader of the workshop dressed in a business suit, standing in a long, dark, Gothic style chapel with a puzzled look on his face. He may have been looking for an electrical outlet or maybe even a good reason for even trying to make a presentation in a room that was also a hallway with people constantly walking through it on the way to somewhere else.

The setting was one of the worst possible for his workshop, and worse yet, the screen that had been promised had not arrived. So, before my eyes the leader went about making the best of this ancient space, moving the TV monitor and the VCR over near this outlet, moving the overhead projector over there near that outlet where he could project against the gray stone wall. Gradually the members of the group gathered and at the appointed time Boomershine began his presentation. More or less, throughout the hour and a half, his visuals were banging from wall to wall. Boomershine was lecturing, commenting, storytelling, impersonating numerous historical styles and dancing around while people from time to time wandered through the room on the way to other rooms with embarrassed expressions on their faces.

Nevertheless, Boomershine had such intensity about him and such intelligence in what he was saying that I became more and more convinced that he was on the right track. Then as the *pièce de résistance* of his presentation, he presented what was to the capstone of his argument—video. He showed a video that had been produced in a local church for use in worship. It looked like any home video to me and left me cold.

Yet, I left the workshop persuaded that Boomershine was on target in his advocacy, and advanced in his understanding. Not merely because of the electronic media he used in his presentation. It was rather the overall effect of a person who cared passionately about his message, had thought it through, and was going by God to use every means at his disposal to communicate it, that won me over. In the end, my hope was fulfilled. Later when I visited the Ginghamsburg United Methodist Church in Ohio where Mike Slaughter and his colleagues lit fires that set churches burning to communicate, I found Tom Boomershine emerging from the production studio.

This remains for me an enduring image of Christian witness in the electronic age. This is what preaching at the party is like. It is saying "Wake up!" in a thousand different images and a sometimes-hoarse voice—"Awake, you sleeper, the kingdom of Heaven is within you!" Some people are going to keep right on sleeping, and others will be passing through on their way to somewhere else. But here and there, someone will be awakened by a hymn, and someone awakened by a video, and someone wakes up to a spoken word, and the congregation is on their feet, not sleepwalking to the edge of a cliff but celebrating. They are celebrating at the center of life with the bread and butter of the people on the table with the Bread and Wine of the Gospel.

Six | Concretion and Transformation

> The substantial citizens of Imperial Rome and the Orthodox Jews of the synagogue looked down on the small tradesmen, fisherman, beggars and the prostitutes who followed Jesus as he preached contempt for the existing order of things. Yet Imperial Rome and the Temple collapsed, while Jesus' followers changed the course of history.
>
> —Rene DuBois[1]

THIS STATEMENT IS ALL the more powerful because it comes from a scientist rather than an apologist who is stressing the truth often ignored—the Christians in the early centuries after Christ actually found ways to live out the challenge presented by Jesus Christ and his apostles to positively change the world. Paul established the vital connection between proclamation, transformation and concretion in his Epistle to the Romans. Having shown in Romans 10 how faith comes by preaching, in Romans 12 Paul challenges them not to conform to their world but to be transformed! Even more daring he challenges them to live out this faith in the concrete situations of daily life. Paul shows how this concrete response by individuals and groups leads to transformation and the transformation supports further concrete response:

> So then, my friends, because of God's great mercy to us I appeal to you: offer yourselves as a living sacrifice to God, dedicated to his service and pleasing to him. This is the true worship that you should offer. Do not be conformed to this world but let God transform you inwardly by a complete change of your mind. Then you will be able to know the will of God—what is good and is pleasing to him and is perfect.

---

1. Dubos, "The New Pessimism"; quoted in Cherry et al., eds., *A Return to Vision*, 5–12.

A closer look at this passage reveals that human activity is a response to God's action in Jesus Christ. We are not initiating some campaign to make things nice in Rome or anywhere else. We are called to make things new. God has offered us a new way of life in Jesus Christ and we are called to offer ourselves back in sacrificial service to God and our neighbor.

Moreover, this service is worship. That's right, *worship*! Worship is not primarily that hour or so set aside on Sunday morning to go to church. Worship is that 24/7 reception of God's gift of life and our offering of ourselves in loving service. That hour or so on Sunday morning is a celebration of that gift with preaching that leads us to a deeper understanding of what it means.

The emphasis of the present work is preaching but it presupposes the Christian community active in everyday life. It has been like this from the beginning as we see for example in the Acts of the Apostles. The Day of Pentecost with its preaching and large crowd was a great day but it was what happened everyday after Pentecost that changed the world. There were four distinct but related activities that became identified as teaching (*didachē*), fellowship (*koinōnia*), breaking of bread (*diakonia*) and worship (*liturgeia*, the work of the people). The early Christians made these actions concrete on a daily basis and the world changed.

We go forth into the world not to conform to it but to transform it and that transformation begins with us individually and collectively. The world has a set of values that are drummed into us constantly, values like—bigger is better, looking good is more important than being good, sex sells, money matters most, etc. We are called to march out into that word to a different drum. The drumbeat is the Will of God. It is the beat of faith and hope and love.

Followers of Christ hope to win other followers not by selling drums but by following His beat in such a way that others want to join the parade. That parade may form in the church, but its line of march is into the streets and homes and offices and meeting places and everywhere people are making the concrete choices that shape life.

Transforming the world is an overwhelming task. It is essential that we recognize the limits of what we can do, but it is also essential not to limit what God can do. The world is changing every moment and we participate in this change in the decisions we make and the actions we do or do not take. When we renew our minds in line with that of Jesus Christ, we are transformed. When we act concretely to love and not hate, have faith and not fear, hope and not despair, the world is transformed.

Concretion is key to transformation as projected in Romans, but other themes are important including comfort and confidence. There is no transformation without conflict and suffering. We do not win all the struggles with injustice, and at times we lose badly.

There is suffering that comes to us, and some suffering we seem to seek on our own.

Paul faces this honestly but states one of the most comforting themes of faith: "In everything God works for good with those who love him, with those who are called according to his purposes" (Romans 8:28). The faith that God is working for good through us when we love Him, even when we cannot see its results is a source of great strength. Many other passages of Scripture support this faith and we are wise to be familiar with them.

Confidence also characterizes the Christian effort of transformation. Is it a struggle? Of course it is. What did we expect when we were invited to take up our cross and follow him, a picnic? Paul never minimizes evil but counsels us to overcome evil with good. He frankly lists enemies but declares, "In all these things we are more than conquerors through Christ who loved us and gave himself for us." For, "If God be for us, who can be against us?"

Our confidence is based not on the conditions of society but on the character of God. In the beginning, God. In the end, God. We face the struggle in its darkest hours as did Jesus Christ, with commitment to God's will. As did Paul, knowing that the sufferings of this present time are not worthy to be compared with the glory that shall be revealed in us. As in Martin Luther King Jr., who went to the mountaintop, and saw the Promised Land that he would not occupy, with the confidence that "We shall overcome." As with the one who gave this prophet his name Martin Luther:

> Though this world with devils filled shall threaten to undo us,
> We will not fear for God hath willed his Truth to triumph
> through us.

The question today is not "Is preaching transformational?" but "How is preaching transformational?" The answer I propose is that preaching is transformational through the process by which human lives individually and collectively are renewed, including the creative process by which words of the Bible are transformed from an ancient text to a contemporary message with concrete expressions.

Transformation occurs as individuals and groups respond concretely to the Gospel. This is one of the paradoxes of preaching. Transformation comes not from elaborate schemes of social engineering trying to change people but by the attitudes and actions of people in their everyday lives.

The accent falls on choice rather than change as such. The change comes from the choices we make. Indeed, trying to change people tends to be counter productive. But where a vision of a better future emerges and the choices that need to be made to realize that vision become clear are followed by the appropriate actions, change occurs.

Transformation encompasses this entire process including divine as well as human activity:

1. Accept the current situation.
2. Envision the alternatives.
3. Make the choices and take the actions to realize the vision.

This process of transformation is essentially the creative process. In the twenty-first century we must use it in relation to a range of issues. Peacemaking remains a issue.

The relationship between concretion and transformation is complex. It is seldom if ever a matter of one directly causing the other. We may see concretion as the microcosm of which transformation is the macrocosm.

William Wagner detects a similar distinction in his study of how Islam plans to change the world. Of these methods Wagner writes that "Generally speaking, they could be classified as Micro (work with individuals and local groups), Metta (work with larger groups and institutions) and Macro (work that attempts to change a whole society and its thinking)."[2] Wagner looks carefully at these dimensions at work. For one thing it draws attention to the fact that whether Christians want to transform the world or not, some Muslims do. They are working hard at this every day and Christians must do no less, in a way that is dialogical rather than destructive. Further, Wagner's distinction of three dimensions of change with Metta (or Meta) mediating between the Micro and the Macro, is illuminating and instructive.

---

2. Wagner, *How Islam Plans to Change the World*, 13.

Concretion and Transformation

Most pastors and congregations are focused on the Micro-the individual and local. This is where most of their interest and energy will be invested. If this is all that concerns them they are likely to become merely microscopic. Therefore attention must also be paid to Macro of world affairs and mission and the restructures, which link them. Such synergy is presupposed in our discussion here.

Preaching can motivate people to act. However, before turning to leading examples, it is important to note that late into the twentieth century influential church leaders and teachers of homiletics were arguing against transformational preaching. Lucy Rose set one popular alternative forth in her book, *Sharing the Word*.

"Transformational Voices Enter the Conversation"—this is how Lucy Rose refers to my work and that of others associated with the New Homiletical movement, wherein she summarizes homiletical theory and practice in the modern era.

That view is challenged by the kerygmatic styles of Barth, Dodd, and others. Rose's description of the work of these major figures, while brief, is on the whole fair. She continues: "I have chosen the term 'transformational' because it conveys the commonly held belief that a sermon should be an experience that transforms the worshiper"[3] Rose then raises a "transformational umbrella," and puts me under it along with the usual suspects Fred Craddock, David Buttrick, and others. This discussion also strikes me as perceptive, indeed appreciative. Rose confesses that this approach to preaching was a positive influence on her, that she is grateful to those who developed it, that it has been a constructive force in her own life and work.

Having acknowledged the positive aspects of transformational preaching, however, Rose rejects it. She concludes that transformational preaching is not effective in changing people's lives, citing the Bishops Committee report of 1982 and others. Further, to accent preaching as "event" puts undue pressure upon preacher and congregation. Rose offers her alternative that she calls "Conversational Preaching."

This turn from transformational preaching appears to have been influential in some homiletical thought and mainline church preaching, with some exceptions into the early twenty-first century. This is unfortunate, because preaching can be at once transformational and conversa-

---

3. Rose, *Sharing the Word*, 59.

tional. Indeed, they reinforce each other as I tried to argue in my earlier work and repeat here. Fortunately, I am not alone in this. John McClure makes this point convincingly in his book *The Roundtable Pulpit: Where Leadership and Preaching Meet*. McClure develops a collaborative approach in which partnership with the congregation is not opposed to leadership but a necessary dimension of it. McClure shows how a "Public Theology of preaching" nourishes and empowers the congregation.[4]

Event and Conversation

Event and conversation are two major terms used to describe preaching. Many pages have appeared in print about these terms and I have written many more trying to get at the heart of the matter.

I conclude that the strength of conversation is that it identifies a genuine element in preaching which connects it to a broad range of human experience. The weakness is that conversation does not identify what is distinctive about preaching. Conversation is such a broad term that it is used in reference to "casual" talk about trivia to the dialogues of Plato.

The strength of event is that it identifies a genuine element in preaching which connects with a broad range of human experience but also has a distinct theological and homiletical reference. The weakness of event is that the word is ambiguous and has connotations that may seem hierarchical and threatening to some.

In recent discussions some have sought to drive a wedge between these terms and their implications as if they were inimical to each other and that preaching must be oriented either toward event or conversation.

That discussion is likely to continue but I believe that the wedge will become a bridge in the Next Homiletics. The continuities between event and conversation are greater than their discontinuities. The event of preaching calls for conversation and conversation without event is merely talk.

To show what I mean let me appeal to ordinary experience and the New Testament, having written at length about homiletical, theological, and historical factors.

In ordinary experience most people detect a difference between small talk and big talk. We detect the difference in preaching. There are sermons that go on and on but get nowhere. And there are sermons that

---

4. McClure, *Roundtable Pulpit*, 13–20.

Concretion and Transformation

get to us. They hit home and we feel as Rilke did when he wrote "You must change your life." That is big talk and it is an event.

Transformation of culture is one of the possibilities explored by H. Richard Niebuhr in his classic work entitled "Christ and Culture" which appeared at the middle of the twentieth century. The author saw the importance of the debate about Christianity and civilization and entered the "double-wrestle" of the church with its Lord and with its society. He carefully considered several distinctive types of approach that he called Christ Against Culture, Christ of Culture, Christ above Culture, Christ and Culture in Paradox and Christ the Transformer of Culture.

The author deals carefully with each of these types and finds that Christ the Transformer of Culture represents "the great central tradition of the church,"[5] which includes the Gospels, Epistles, Augustine, Tolstoy, Ritchsl, Kierkegaard and Maurice. This view acknowledges the radical distinction between God's work in Christ and man's work in culture but is distinguished from dualists because of its more positive and hopeful attitude toward culture.

For H. Richard Niebuhr, Augustine is himself an example of the meaning of the conversion of culture: "Christ is the transformer of culture for Augustine in the sense that he dies, reinvigorates, and regenerates that life of man, expressed in all human works, which in present actuality is the perverted and confuted essence of a fundamentally good nature."[6] Niebuhr in this work and others I take to be a rich resource for transformation in the twenty-first century. The theological grounding of transformation as the church's calling is solid, although we may differ at some points and need to add fresh examples from the intervening years.

I say this recognizing that some reaction against Richard Niebuhr in the latter part of the twentieth century supported the homiletical turn away from transformation. For example, Stanley Hauerwas and William Willimon wrote: "We have come to believe that few books have been a greater hindrance to an accurate assessment of our situation than *Christ and Culture*."[7] These authors state flatly that Niebuhr failed and contributed in a major way to what is wrong.

---

5. H. Richard Niebuhr, *Christ and Culture*, 190.
6. Ibid., 209.
7. Hauerwas and Willimon, *Resident Aliens*, 32.

Frankly, I do not recognize Niebuhr's work in this caricature of it. Moreover, the "radical alternative" they propose, which equates Reinhold Niebuhr with Jerry Falwell and chooses Jerry Falwell as the model to emulate, is unconvincing to say the least.[8]

At issue here is whether or not Christian preaching roots in Christ the transformer of culture and is therefore legitimately transformational. There are other points of view that tended to turn preaching and homiletics away from this task in the late-twentieth century. It will be up to those preaching now and in the future to decide their course.

The transformational stone rejected by some in the establishment has become the cornerstone of revolutionary preaching in the twenty-first century. Church leaders across the theological and political spectrum who recognize that we must be transformed by the power of God, worship, and preaching are powerful instruments of love and justice. To conform to this world of war, poverty, disease and ignorance and violence is not an option for churches, individuals, groups and nations.

Rick Warren of Saddleback Community Church is one outstanding example of how preaching and transformation become real today. These themes are at the heart of his ministry based in the congregation and reaching around the world in best selling books, savvy media use and action programs. We have already noted the "Primacy of Preaching" in Warren's ministry. Transformation is at the heart of this ministry and preaching.

"The truth transforms us," Warren writes, quoting John 8:31–32, "If you continue in my word, then are you my disciples indeed; and you shall know the truth and the truth shall make you free."

"Be you transformed by the renewing of your minds" is how Paul's direction to the Romans begins. Warren writes: "No other habit can do more to transform your life and make you more like Jesus than daily reflection on Scripture. As we take the time to contemplate God's truth, seriously reflecting on the example of Christ, we are 'transformed into his likeness with ever increasing glory'" (2 Corinthians 3:18 NIV).[9]

All of our contemplation, reading and reflection on the Word are useless if we do not apply them to our daily lives. We must be "doers of the word" (James 1:22 KJV). Warren admits that this is the hardest step of

---

8. Ibid., 69–71.
9. Warren, *The Purpose-Driven Life*, 190.

all, but urges that we take it by writing out an action step as a result of our Bible reading and study: "This action step should be *personal* (involving *you*), *practical* (something you can *do*), and *provable* (with a deadline to it). Every application will involve either your relationship to God, your relationship to others, or your personal character."[10]

Being doers of the Word is not a simple possibility. In fact, the next chapter in Warren's book is titled "Transformed by Trouble." To be a doer of the Word will get us into trouble in a world full of problems. Yet behind every problem there is a purpose. When we discover that purpose, we also discover that "in all things God works for the good of those who love him, who have been called according to his purpose" (Romans 8:28 NIV).

Preaching the truth transforms us and empowers us to participate in the transformation of the world by the Grace of God. This simple truth is fundamental to the complex ministry of Rick and Kay Warren and the community through which millions of people all over the world are finding God's purpose in their lives.

Jim Wallis is another leader who is demonstrating how preaching leads to concrete actions that can contribute to major social transformation. From his experience as a local pastor and international activist, Wallis is showing a way to relate faith and politics that is moving religious and political leaders to a new Great Awakening. Wallis's *The Great Awakening* is one of a series of best-selling books that spell out both the *why* and the *how* to change the world.

Why we seek to change the world is of great importance. Wallis writes approvingly of Bishop N. T. Wright of Durham that:

> Wright understands that the real political questions for Christians are always questions of worship: who or what is finally 'Lord' for us, here does the ultimate majority lie, what is God like, and therefore how are we to live in the world? Wright says, "The key to mission is always worship. You can only be reflecting the love of God into the world if you are worshipping the true God who creates the world out of overpowering, self-giving love. The more you look at that God and celebrate that love, the more you have to be reflecting that overflowing, self-giving love into the world." What a radical political alternative that is—a kingdom defined by

---

10. Ibid., 191–92.

the power of love definitely not from the world but emphatically for the world."[11]

On this basis Wallis sets forth Rules of Engagement by which faith can become involved with politics without being usurped by politics:

- God hates injustice.
- The kingdom of God is a new order.
- The church is an alternative community.
- The kingdom of God transforms the world by addressing the specifics of injustice.
- The church is the conscience of the state, holding it accountable for upholding justice and restraining its violence.
- Take a global perspective.
- Seek the common good.[12]

The *why* and the *how* of changing the world through faith are developed in concrete ways in the book and the movement of The Great Awakening. More than a book, it is an invitation, like the Gospel itself to repent and believe and take part in the Kingdom of God.

Christianity and the Social Crisis in the 21st Century is especially important because it links the classic by Walter Rauschenbusch to this century though the labors of his grandson, Paul Rauschenbush. Paul, in turn, has called on a number of leaders to relate the salient features of the original to the new situation, including Tony Campolo on the "Social Aims of Jesus," and James Forbes Jr. on "Sounding the Trumpet Today: Changing Lives and Redeeming the Soul of Society in the 21st Century."

Martin Luther King Jr. said that Rauschenbusch's original was a book that left an indelible imprint on his thinking. Reading it again we can see why it inspired Dr. King and connects those of us working in the twenty-first century with the enduring contributions of those who have passed the torch to us. With all that is new in our context there is much to be learned from Dr. King and other leaders with a twentieth-century legacy.

Martin Luther King Jr. is a major bridge between the transformational preaching of the twentieth and twenty-first centuries. This bridge

11. Wallis, *Great Awakening,* 56.
12. Ibid., 61.

function that is widely recognized is especially vivid for me because of its association with the Edmund Pettis Bridge in Selma, Alabama, to which I marched with Dr. King in 1965. We had gathered at Browns Chapel in Selma to worship, sing, pray and listen to Dr. King and others preach. This was very different from the March on Washington at which I had heard Dr. King in 1963. There had been hundreds of thousands in Washington, but there were only hundreds in Selma. The dream of Dr. King was facing the nightmare of segregation. Was that dream to die in Selma where those who had attempted to cross that bridge and march to Montgomery had been beaten back and bloodied on the previous Sunday? Or would we dare to march again?

Dr. King preached and we marched. This was to become known as "Turnaround Tuesday," for although we stopped at the bridge to pray and bear witness, and returned to the chapel, that action prepared the way for the next leg of the march that went all the way from Selma to Montgomery and the passage of that landmark legislation known as the high water mark of the Civil Rights Movement.

Dr. King's preaching was transformational because he spoke it not only to huge mall in Washington, but to the little church in Selma. The response of those in that little church marched the dream back to Washington in the form of legislation that changed lives forever. *Words that Changed a Nation* was the title of a documentary on Dr. King done by CNN. We can see now that CNN was right in acknowledging the national and international impact of Dr. King's preaching. But the documentary was also accurate in referring not only to the "I Have a Dream Speech" in Washington, but to the handwritten sermons of King's seminary days, the pastoral ministry in Montgomery, his leadership in the Bus Boycott, the Letter from Birmingham Jail, and all those sermons in cathedral churches and little chapels like that in Selma.

Dr. King deserves to be celebrated on special days and in many ways. We still have much to learn from him and his colleagues on the bridge to the future. Much of that will be learned by the students now in schools and the pastors of little chapels and those who are crossing the bridges of bigotry because they too have a dream.

This leads to Reinhold Niebuhr, a great theologian of the twentieth century who began as a pastor in Detroit and went on to become internationally acclaimed as a scholar and political leader. To my generation of theological students, Niebuhr inspired us to enact faith publicly while acknowledging the limits of all human endeavors. Reinhold Niebuhr's name is seldom invoked now but his influence is more widespread than any other theologian. For Reinhold Niebuhr is the author of what is known as "The Serenity Prayer":

> The Serenity Prayer
> God, give us grace to accept with serenity
> the things that cannot be changed,
> Courage to change the things
> which should be changed,
> and the Wisdom to distinguish
> the one from the other.
>
> Living one day at a time,
> Enjoying one moment at a time,
> Accepting hardship as a pathway to peace,
> Taking, as Jesus did,
> This sinful world as it is,
> Not as I would have it,
> Trusting that you will make all things right,
> If I surrender to your will,
> So that I may be reasonably happy in this life,
> And supremely happy with You forever in the next.
> Amen.

It may seem a long way from Niebuhr and his "Serenity Prayer" to the scenic but often troubled streets of San Francisco, but Cecil Williams and Glide Memorial United Methodist Church made that move in Twelve Steps. Niebuhr's prayer became a hallmark of the Twelve Step Program of Alcoholics Anonymous, which expanded into the broader Recovery Movement. Pastor Cecil Williams and the Glide community found in this movement a way to transform a struggling church and a suffering people. In his book entitled *No Hiding Place*, Williams spells out the "Spirituality and Practice of Recovery," which has drawn national and international attention. There is much to be learned from this approach that connects personal and social transformation.

Concretion is the process whereby the meaning of the biblical text is brought to expression in the situation of the hearers. This process is brought about in the sermon by suggestions of concrete personal and social responses that are intended by the text, although by definition the process moves beyond the explicitly sermonic. There is thus a continu-

Concretion and Transformation

ity between confirmation and concretion. Confirmation is itself a form of concretion when the act of understanding takes place for the hearer. Concretion in other forms is not completely distinct from the act of understanding but is precisely the living out of that understanding. The distinction is made here to advance the discussion within homiletics dealing with the interaction between what is said on Sunday and what is to be lived the rest of the week. Confirmation emphasizes the "hearing," and concretion stresses the "doing," although both are acts of obedience to the Word—following Jesus' utterance that men are to "hear" and to "do" his word (see Matthew 7:24–29 and Luke 6:47–49). Concretion is concerned with participation in what has been said as the hearer carries it forth into his life, and it is obviously of great importance to dynamic preaching which swings into revolution.

The Irony of History

Only when this point of orientation is clear can we properly speak of what the sermon does by way of concretion. For we are dealing here with a great irony—preaching that made no claims for itself has profoundly altered the course of history.

Luther had his critics, of course. "Is preaching worth it?" they sneered. Luther replied that if a single person were comforted by the Gospel, it would be worth it if the whole earth should shake. Here is the irony—that Luther, who asked nothing but that the word of God be heard, is a pivot on which the history of the modern world turns.

We see this irony in the apostolic preachers, who, making no claim for themselves and with no wealth but their words, "turned the world upside down." We see it again in John Wesley, whose decision to preach in the fields of England was, as the historian Lecky said, one of the events that saved the British Isles from a bloody revolution. It is the irony of the God who has given us his word in the carpenter from Nazareth, Jesus Christ.

How has Christian preaching so dramatically shaped history? "Repentance" is the keynote of the Christian preaching which has the effect of changing the course of history. To repent means to turn from the kingdoms of this world to the kingdom of God. To repent means to turn toward the new age being brought in by Jesus Christ and to worship him alone as Lord. Having affirmed the lordship of Jesus Christ, the

Christian can never again relax under tyrannies which seek "to lord it over" others.[13]

Attitude and Act

It is at the level of *attitude* rather than at the level of program that the Christian Gospel fundamentally strikes. How does one *dispose* himself toward his brother, his neighbor, and a stranger? What is his *attitude* toward himself, his God, and his world? The question of attitude is the primary question. This is the undercurrent issue to be addressed in preaching, even as the current issues change shape.

Christianity becomes precisely "a beautiful lie" when its significance is expressed only in terms of basic attitudes and general principles which do not come to grips with the actual tyrannies under which people live. Racial segregation existing alongside thriving churches is only one example of how effectively we have learned to tell such a lie. While generations of African-Americans were all but stripped of their humanity, churchmen comforted themselves with the thought of how much they "loved" their slaves. Only recently have some begun to see that sentimental love is a lie. Love becomes truth in the concrete only when it expresses itself in the search for justice.

The Range of Responsibility

It may be asked, how can preaching be biblical and at the same time deal with "the total dimension of human life?" The question, though common enough, is misconceived. The real question is, how can preaching be biblical *without* dealing with the total dimension of life?

It is true that repentance does not lead to a specific program of social action, and that the consequences of the attitude of love are not always spelled out in full detail in the Bible. Yet preaching which is faithful to the intention of the biblical text will inevitably speak to man's personal social life because in the Bible, repentance, this turning toward God and the neighbor, is always portrayed in the context of one's relationships to others and in the context of the realities of institutional life. Biblical faith calls man to accept the full range of his responsibility. The Bible literally abounds in passages dealing with the responsibility of man for his broth-

---

13. Michalson, *Hinge of History*, 244–45.

er—and not only in terms of the one-to-one relationship of individuals but also in terms of the social structures.

Preaching is not the simple reiteration of the ethical demands of the Bible. Rather, acquaintance with biblical studies and the field of social ethics is presupposed so that the preacher can enter into a process of critical analysis which will yield the significance of the deepest intention of the Bible as it comes to bear on the personal-social structures of the contemporary scene.

Preaching attempts to phrase suggestions of personal-social responses intended by the text. These phrasings tend to fall into two basic groups, direct and indirect.

Direct Approaches

The preacher may elicit the response of his or her hearers by going directly to the point and speaking in as straightforward a manner as possible. Sermons on "social issues" generally fall into this category. The preacher engages with a social problem and seeks to bring the best of biblical faith and of contemporary thinking to its solution.

Indirect Approaches

The preacher may elicit the response of his or her hearers by indirect approaches which follow a less obvious course but which arrive at the goal with more of a revelatory quality and with greater impact. These statements appear in sermons that deal with concern about a great theological insight developed by biblical faith and Christian history.

The need for *direct* statement is clear, undeniable, and often effective, as we have seen. Such statements tend to be most effective when they are occasional.

Dynamic preaching, as here understood, most enthusiastically sponsors indirect statements as the most effective way to bring texts to expression *in the long run*. Indeed, one of the most distinctive features about dynamic preaching is that concern for persons in society must be an element in every sermon. Every true sermon is a sermon on *the* social issue—persons in relationship—although it may be only occasionally that a whole sermon is directed to a specific social issue. The imperative character of this claim should be underscored. The sermon should intend that the biblical text come to expression in the lives of the hearers.

This is not just an addendum to the sermon; it is part of the sermon *by definition*.

Where concretion is lacking we do not merely find a poor sermon; we find no sermon at all. It is not *primarily* in order to influence history that the sermon deals with men in their concreteness. The terrain of time may be shaped by such preaching, yes, but the primary basis for such preaching is that the Bible itself *intends* such preaching, in which the claim of God is seen in the concrete context of the claims of men. Our point is that social concern is so inherently a part of the Bible that no sermon that does not share this concern is consistent with its text.

At the same time, the indirect approach is likely to be more effective in realizing the biblical intention to elicit response. Preaching like this does not attempt to "whip up the will" but to stir the imagination. This preaching attempts to unfold the meaning of the text in such a way that we see our brothers and sisters in a new light. Preaching may not "tell us" to love our brother, but may so reveal our brother to us that such advice is superfluous. Preaching that is not the voicing of social directives but a "revelatory experience" is most likely to bring the meaning of the text to expression in the lives of our hearers.

In summing up this part of our discussion, we must draw attention to: (1) the need for depth study in the field of ethics; and (2) the need for involvement in the community. Only as the preacher engages in the depth study of the ethical situation of contemporary man is he able to penetrate to the heart of man's dilemmas and to avoid that shallow topicality which makes him a mere commentator on the news of the day. Such study should familiarize him with the underling realities of the choices before us and engender a willingness to help people work out the details. Outstanding in this regard is Charles L. Campbell's *The Word before the Powers: An Ethic of Preaching*, Walter Wink's series of books on confronting the Powers, and Arthur Van Seter's *Preaching as a Social Act: Theology and Practice*.

As important as the word from the pulpit is, one must never suppose that it exhausts the preacher's opportunity or responsibility. The preacher who really cares about the world cares constantly, and is involved inevitably in the quest for love and justice in the midst of life. He or she will counsel individuals, serve on committees, initiate projects, sponsor forums on public issues, move to the centers of power in the community, will demonstrate in every way possible that because *God* cares about man in his myriad relationships, God's minister cares too. Moreover, this minister will develop a strategy that weighs the effectiveness of means of influence open to them. While preaching on social issues is often a way of being responsible, it can become in some instances the best way of actually avoiding the brunt of a problem. There may be times to speak softly in the pulpit but loudly in city hall. Above all, preachers must know that they stand under the judgment and mercy of the God whose message they proclaim.

The preacher as the servant of the word may be used by God to alter the shape of history. This happens when through sermons the meaning of the biblical text is made concrete in the lives of our hearers. Yet we must be careful not to turn the chancel into a parade ground where we shout out commands to the recruits. The power of the Gospel is not the power of the military. It is the power of the Holy Spirit who is symbolized not by the warlike eagle but by the gentle dove.

The Christian preacher is sensitive to the irony of history whereby his or her great power lies precisely in the fact that he or she has little power. The power that we serve is that of God who embodied his power in the carpenter, Jesus of Nazareth. Yet it is faith in Jesus Christ that overcomes the world.

Consider Paul, the preacher, before Felix, the governor. Anyone seeing this encounter would hardly have given the Christian a chance for his life. On one hand stood Felix, governor of the province, with legions of soldiers at his command, with the power of the Roman Empire behind his throne. On the other hand stood Paul, a crippled Jew, alone pleading the cause of Christ.

The way of the Christian revolution is the long way around the quiet path of love. It has its drama and its battles, but they are embraced by the arms of sacrifice and toil. Christians are called to the tough task of expressing their faith in the midst of the concrete encounters of their lives.

Malcolm Gladwell provides many examples of how concretion leads to transformation in his influential book, *The Tipping Point*. He looks carefully at how the crime rate was reduced in New York, for example, and observes that a number of things were changing incrementally, but there was one dramatic moment when "everything can change all at once" which he calls the Tipping Point. Gladwell supports this view with evidence from many sources, some of which have special relevance for this study.

He reports a study at Princeton University on how Princeton Seminary students came to enact the Parable of the Good Samaritan. The evidence Gladwell gives in support of the argument for how movements get started especially struck me. The example he gives is John Wesley, who preached throughout England and organized small groups who met regularly and stood for something:

> In the late eighteenth and early nineteenth centuries, for example, the Methodist movement became epidemic in England and North America, tipping from 20,000 to 90,000 followers in the U.S. in the space of five or six years in the 1780s ... This was a group, in other words, that stood for something. Over the course of his life, Wesley traveled ceaselessly among these groups, covering as much as four thousand miles a year by horseback, reinforcing the tenets of the Methodist belief. He was a classic Connector ... Wesley realized that if you wanted to bring a fundamental change in people's belief and behavior, a change that would persist and serve as an example to others, you needed to create a community around them, where those new beliefs could be practiced and expressed and nurtured ... What most underlie successful epidemics, in the end, is a bedrock belief that change is possible, the people can radically transform their behavior or beliefs in the face of the right kind of impetus.[14]

This belief is at the heat of preaching that transforms.

What Comes Next?

What comes next for the sermon? In one sense we refer to the immediate liturgical context. Here the answer may come in a prayer, the creed, a hymn, and a call to Christian discipleship, a service of healing, Holy Communion, or some combination of these. This immediate response is very important and deserves serious attention on the part of the preacher and everyone planning worship. What comes right after the sermon can help the hearer take the message home or leave it undelivered. The end of the sermon is critical because it is the beginning of the active response of the congregation and every preacher and church must find ways to make this transition work.

After the liturgy itself is complete, the question arises again: What comes next? How does our worship and preaching relate to our everyday

---

14. Gladwell, *Tipping Point*, 172–73, and 258.

life? This involves what we may call midrange consequences that enable preacher and congregation to interact for members to have fellowship, study or social action together.

The preacher herself or himself will be available to those in the congregation who wish to speak person-to-person. These interactions, though brief, can clear up a point or affirm a connection. In addition, the truly communicative preacher will find ways to be viable for further conversations either by appointment or stated hours.

The preacher is attentive to other follow-up activities, although others may take on the arrangements and details. The preacher may make reference to information and materials or opportunities for response. Churches that have a significant impact on their community make the most of combining fellowship, education, and tabling. "Tabling" has become virtually an art form today. It involves people working a table in the meeting room to share information and materials that help the visitor to take the next step.

"What comes next?" These immediate responses lead us to the long-range question of the ultimate goal of worship and preaching. The answer, whether arising from elaborate argument or a leap of faith, is the Kingdom of God, the reign of God. This is the rule of God in obedience to the divine will as prayed for by Jesus to "Our Father in Heaven, thy kingdom come, thy will be done on earth as it is in heaven..." To pray this prayer is to commit ourselves to do that will daily, concretely.

As St. Augustine said, the end of all our action is to participate in the kingdom that has no end.

Seven | Conclusion

IN CONCLUSION WE OFFER a brief summary, an E-Mail Epistle to local pastors (note the Next Homiletics), suggest ways to grow in preaching, and share a final word.

In his *Letters and Papers from Prison,* Dietrich Bonhoeffer imagined that the day will come when men, women, and children will once more be called to communicate the word of God so that the world will be changed and renewed. It will be a new language, verbal and visual, dialogical and digital, challenging, but also liberating and redeeming, as was Jesus's language. It will shock some and yet overcome them by its power. It will be the language of a new righteousness and truth proclaiming the Good News of God's presence with us in this world as Creator, Redeemer, and Transformer.

This is the twenty-first century, and I say, that day is *now.*

Summing Up

Our exploration discovers that the renewal of preaching is taking place in the twenty-first century and holds great promise of transforming it with the Next Homiletics. We have seen that a communications revolution is sweeping through the churches leaving some on fire and others burned out. This work shows what makes the difference and how that can empower Christian communicators locally and globally.

The Next Homiletics combines Deep Faith and High Tech here to deepen devotion to God and widen service to humanity. Let me be clear: the most effective preachers will master the traditional forms of spoken and written word plus new media formats. There are two challenges for which the preacher of the twenty-first century must be prepared. One comes when he or she has a variety of multimedia available to communicate and must use them effectively. The other comes when the media break down in technical difficulties and he or she must stand there with nothing but their living presence and voice to speak. Never forget that the most effective multimedia communication ever created is the human being.

The promise of preaching has never been greater than it is early in the twenty-first century as seen in the signs of hope identified here. Yet the perils of preaching have never been greater also and these must be faced honestly. Beginning with a review of the situation today, we proceeded step-by-step through the preparation and presentation of the sermon leading to transformation. The sermon in the local parish is seen as the microcosm of the macrocosm that is the communication of God's good news.

This work explores ways to maximize the promise of preaching and confront challenges leading to transformation. We affirm those who are involved in this movement and invite others to launch into the deep waters that challenge, cleanse and change the world.

An E-Mail Epistle

While preparing this book I have also been preaching and teaching and in regular contact with other clergy and laity. I am happy to report that I have communicated on the Internet with pastors who have e-mailed me for help. They have shared sermons with me, raised questions and I have done my best to study the sermons and give feedback. Bill and Lynn Willis—a clergy couple who both preach—and I had an extensive exchange. After we had done this for some time, I wrote this to summarize what I had tried to share with them, in effect, the subject of this book.

From Desperate Preachers to Dynamic Preaching

There are some desperate preachers these days. Something is missing from their sermons. They know it. Their people know it. I know it because they tell me so.

When I look and listen I often find strengths in their work. They do really want to communicate. Most sense the importance of preaching biblically. They want to be helpful. But something is missing.

What is missing most of the time is the dynamic element that connects the factors in the sermon into a living experience. It's like when the lights go out. What is wrong? Is it the bulb? The lamp? The fuse? You have to check out the system and be sure that the electrical force is running through the complete circuit to turn on the light.

The factors in the circuit of dynamic preaching may be identified like this:

1. Commitment
2. Concern
3. Connection
4. Confirmation
5. Construction
6. Communication
7. Commission

Check it out on your own preaching.

Commitment

Commitment means that you are dedicated to communicating the Gospel with all your heart and soul and mind and strength. The sermon is a message from the heart of the preacher to the heart of the congregation about the heart of God.

Concern

Be clear about the one major concern, burden, and heart of your message. Jesus was. The Bible is. Be able to state this simply and clearly "The kingdom of heaven is within you." Say with St. Augustine, "What concerns me here is . . ." Say, "The good news today is . . ." I heard a sermon recently in which the preacher had eleven points. And that was just the children's sermon! If there were one point, I might have remembered it.

Connect

Connect the word of the Bible with the words of the congregation. What are they telling you? What are they worried about? What are they hoping for? Where are they hurting? What are they saying by their actions, their gestures, and their postures?

Confirm

Strengthen the message with stories and poems from daily life, popular culture, and classical culture.

Construct

Gather the materials into a meaningful shape. Open with a clear statement of concern. Build with confirmations. Close with a restatement of the concern. Vary the forms. The sermon may take the form of the story, a poem, a dialogue, a PowerPoint presentation, a short video or film, or many other forms.

Communicate

Be alive. Share your feelings as well as your thoughts. Look at people when you talk to them. Find the faces that come alive and speak to them. Speak clearly. If you are using a new form of communication, tell then people why.

Commission

Send the people forth into the world and go with them.

Check this out for yourself. This approach is simple enough to flash a light on any sermon and complex enough to illuminate you for a lifetime.

Recently I checked back with them to see if our Internet seeds had sprung up or withered away. I was grateful to hear that both Lynn and Bill were positive in their replies. They identified specific ways that had been helpful and noted areas for further growth. Lynn said that my words had given her courage and Bill told me that my advice had given him more joy in preaching.

If anything I have learned, and communicated electronically, or any other way, brings courage and joy to preachers and their congregations, I thank God.

The Next Homiletics

The Next Homiletics combines Deep Faith and High Tech to deepen devotion to God and service to humanity. Deep Faith is grounded on the Bible and the life of the Church. Sources include primarily St. Augustine, Martin Luther, John Wesley, Karl Barth, Rudolf Bultmann, Paul Tillich, Gerhard Ebeling, Carl Michalson, and a host of artists and angels.

This homiletics will be dialogical and digital, employing technology and media, old and new, to prepare, present and communicate.

The Next Homiletics includes the following elements defined above and related dynamically. With eventfulness as the distinctive core, these elements constitute the paradigm of the Next Homiletics. Eventfulness, as we define it in this work, is a multi-layered structure, including, but larger than, any single event. The eventfulness arises in the quality of interaction. The goal of homiletics is not to strive for an effect, but to do the work that gives rise to the event of faith.

Paradigm, as I use the word here, is in the technical sense defined by Thomas Kuhn in scientific revolutions rather than the common usage of "model." For Kuhn, a paradigm consists of a distinctive element of emphasis and a framework that embodies the distinction.[1]

Growth in Preaching

"That was a great sermon!" Fran, the woman who said this to me as we shook hands after the service seemed genuinely moved. Then she caught herself and added, "Not every Sunday, but every once in awhile you preach a great sermon." She wanted to encourage me, but not too much.

Every now and then it all comes together, and the preparation pays off in a sermon that lifts clouds of darkness with a power and light filling the sanctuary and spilling out into the neighborhood. How can the power and light that bursts forth in a transforming way on occasion become more constant in preaching? I have sought to share some answers, but learning to preach is a lifelong adventure.

For Chaucer's words remain true for preaching as well as for writing:

> The life so short
> The craft, so long to learn.

I quoted these lines in my earlier work, and in rewriting it have been delighted that Chaucer himself added to them in his "The Parliament of Fowles." I paraphrase:

> For out of old fields come new crops from year to year;
> and out of old books in good faith comes new learning.

---

1. Kuhn, *Structure of Scientific Revolutions*, 1970.

It is good to know that the master who promised that the learning would be life-long also promised that it had benefits.

It is clear that the "marks" of dynamic preaching as set forth in this work are most effective not as rules which are to be rigidly applied, but as guidelines within which creative activity can most effectively take place. In this way, the characteristics of dynamic preaching serve as "canons of criticism," as well as creative stimuli. Hopefully, over a period of time, the way of preaching set forth here will become a vital part of the preacher's theological method. This outline could well serve the preacher as a guide to preparing and evaluating his sermons. Our fundamental question is, "What *happens* in this sermon?" This raises the questions of: What is the intention of the text? The concern of the sermon? What did the preacher do that helped or hindered the evocation of the event? The phenomenon under discussion is the sermon itself—the interaction of preacher and congregation—and norms and structures are referred to as they illuminate this phenomenon. The discussion is sermon-centered rather than rule-centered. Moreover, it is person-centered rather than proposition-centered. The setting is more like that of a discussion group that might normally follow a sermon in church rather than an autopsy following an operation that failed. In this way, the preacher's capacity to relate to others is more fully revealed, and this opens the way to a deeper discussion of why communication did or did not take place. The discussions are not group counseling, but group dynamics are at work, and by raising them to the level of discussion, the student may profit more deeply than from discussions that touch only the surface of abstract principles.

Individual conferences between student and teacher are further helpful, as are special projects that allow "space" to develop the aspects of preaching that matter most to the preacher. Yet even when all these and other methods are put to work, the goal is to have the preacher become so deeply interested and motivated that he or she will continue the creative quest for real preaching. He or she will learn before long to paraphrase the artist Hokusai and say, "If I live to be ninety, perhaps I will learn to preach."

Guidelines for Preparation and Assessment

The marks of dynamic preaching used throughout this work provide useful guidelines in my work as a pastor and teacher. Here is an example of a sermon work sheet for preparation and evaluation. For preparation of course the questions are directed to oneself, and for evaluation to the work of the other, student or colleague.

Preacher: _____ Text: _____
Sermon Title: _____ Date and Location:_____

1. What is the CONCERN of this sermon (heart, purpose, intention?)?
2. How will the preacher CONNECT the text with the congregation (contact, plug in, introduce)?
3. How will the preacher CONFIRM material (support, ingrain, illustrate)?
4. What CONCRETIONS for TRANSFORMATION will be called for (issues, choices, responses, applications)?
5. What CONSTRUCTION or COMPOSITION will the preacher employ (outline, storyboard, script as CLASSIC or CONTEMPORARY FORM)?
6. What COMMUNICATION form or forms will the preacher choose (oral and kinesthetic acts, and/or computer graphics, PowerPoint, iMovie, etc.)?
7. How will the preacher FOLLOW UP (Immediate availability for discussion? Provision of material and opportunities for study? Reference to Action group in church or community, etc.? What have I learned which will help me in my next sermon)?

My concern in all this from my student days through my parish experience and once again in teaching is to relate the central concerns of the Christian faith to the central issues of our time. This means facing the central concerns of our time in the light of Christian faith. This has unfolded not by a preconceived plan but by following my vocation through the stages along life's way. It is a privilege to exercise this vocation in the company of others whose voices and visions so challenge and enrich my own.

Together we may challenge and enrich the world.

Conclusion

So I invite you, the reader, and all my colleagues, to come and stand on the horizon. Let us dream our dreams and share our visions and open our hearts. Let us do more fully in the future than we have in the past. I invite you to vision with me and to find the vehicles for our visions.

What do you see on the horizon of homiletics? What do you hope for? How do we get there?

Lay preaching will grow in importance in the 21st Century for a variety of reasons. One reason is that many lay preachers bring great gifts to this task. C.S. Lewis is a conspicuous example. Another reason is that there will be a greater need to call on them to preach as numbers of ordained clergy decrease. Above all, history shows that God's call to preach is not limited to the ordained clergy, however important they are. The Wesleyan Revival relied heavily on Lay Preachers and the United Methodist Church today is among those with strong programs for them. Therefore, more attention to the nurture, training, and deployment of lay preachers is called for.

Why Preaching Matters

Preaching matters because people live or die from it every day. Without its wisdom, people go over the edge of anxiety and despair. With its power, they are turned to the center of love and hope.

Jesus Christ is at the center of preaching and by the grace of God as Creator, Redeemer and Sustainer, it reaches out to every edge of life where people hurt and hope.

Oriented to eternity, it is looked upon as foolishness by the fashionable. Those who preach must not expect to become rich or famous but will find their reward in being called to be messengers of God.

Why Homiletics Matters

Homiletics matters because preachers live or die by it. Homiletics reveals why they preach and teaches them how.

Homiletics is the art and science of the homily, a form of communication that is unique in that it clams to bear the Word of God in human words and acts. Homiletics is theology in action where the rubber of reflection hits the road of reality.

Homiletics is to preaching what architecture is to construction with the exception that in this case the architect is the construction worker, who must live in the house that is built along with the community.

If preaching is foolishness, homiletics is utter absurd. But it is God's joke and joy for those who get it.

Our situation is like that of the mother who was trapped with her two infant children in a burning building in Brooklyn. They were on the tenth floor but the ladders of the fire department could reach only to the ninth floor. There seemed to be no hope as the flames roared around them. A courageous firefighter climbed to the top of the ladder and tied his legs to the metal frame to gain greater height. He called to the mother of the children that her children and she could be saved, if they could all stretch themselves to the maximum extent. The mother went to the children and said, "We are going to have an adventure!" With that spirit she stretched as far as she could, the fireman stretched as far as he could, and all were saved.

Fires still burn in Brooklyn and Baghdad and elsewhere including Bethlehem. At times Salvation seems far off and the Prince of Peace homeless again. And yet if followers of Jesus Christ stretch themselves to the limits for peace and justice and those of other faiths do the same, our children and we may be saved.

It is of major importance that those of Deep Faith and those in High Tech reach out toward one another to the fullest so that the greatest truth may be shared with the most people. And then from the burning buildings may emerge new life.

This much is sure about renewal in the 21st Century: We are going to have an adventure!

Benediction

In the beginning of this work I quoted the prayer I offer before my sermons. At the end, I give the Benediction based on Paul that I use at the close of the service of worship.

> "Go forth in your adventure of faith,
> And may the Grace of our Lord Jesus Christ,
> The Love of God,
> And the fellowship of the Holy Spirit
> Be with you always
> As they are right now. Amen."

Commentary

ROBERT STEPHEN REID

IN 1998 DAVID RANDOLPH invited me to write an extended introduction to the re-issue of *The Renewal of Preaching*, and he has invited me to provide a concluding commentary for this new edition.[1] I suspect that he asked me to write that 1998 introduction as a result of conversations we had based on two essays I published in the mid-1990's.[2] In both articles I had used the phrase "New Homiletic" more as a noun, naming what I saw as a bounded, describable movement in the field of homiletics. Prior use of the phrase had been more adjectival, pointing to variety in recent homiletic methodologies.[3] Randolph had grounded his proposal of method in the larger concerns of the theology of the New Hermeneutic arguing for a New Homiletic based on the New Hermeneutic. He was especially interested in the New Hermeneutic's conception of human language as the medium of divine *eventfulness* applied to preaching. It provided homileticians with theological language to describe an encounter with God as something other than an aesthetic, or worse, an emotive experience.[4] And it was this parallelism

---

1 Reid, "Introduction." For full references to all citations, see Works Cited at the end of the essay.

2. Reid, et al., "Preaching as the Creation of an Experience"; and Reid, "Postmodernism and the Function of the New Homiletic in Post-Christendom Congregations," 1–13. Our conversations occurred, in part, because I had missed the centrality of *Renewal*'s role in defining New Homiletic as a movement, a lacuna I have sought to remedy subsequently in my published assessments of it in Hogan and Reid, *Connecting with the Congregation*, 25–26; Reid, "Exploring Preaching's Voices from *Ex Cathedra* to Exilic," 138; and Reid, *Four Voices of Preaching*, 121–22.

3. This was especially true of Richard Eslinger, *New Hearing*, 13–14.

4. Randolph, *Renewal of Preaching*, 17. Cf. Ebeling, *Word and Faith*; idem, *The Nature*

of deriving homiletic understanding from a bounded, classifiable approach to theology that provided the basis of more recent claims that it was Randolph who first envisioned a New Homiletic movement that would transcend his own contribution to it.

One of New Homiletic's leading voices, Gene Lowry, was an early adopter of this assessment. In 2001 he wrote, "I have often said that Fred Craddock kicked in the door leading into a whole new preaching era when *As One Without Authority* appeared in 1971. But it was David Randolph who in 1969 named the room beyond the door—calling it the 'New Homiletic.'"[5] In a recent compendium of critical terms in homiletics, John McClure affirms this claim, classifying New Homiletic as "a homiletic movement dating from the late 1960's through mid-1980s that turned away from rational-cognitive models of homiletics and pursued homiletic models grounded in dialogue, narrative, induction, and imagination." He also affirms that David Randolph's *The Renewal of Preaching* should be credited as the source for the movement's name.[6] Perhaps even more than Fred Craddock's *As One Without Authority*, it was *Renewal* that articulated the core features others would expand later as the movement developed.[7] Both Craddock and Lowry were associated with preaching models that reframed the question of how sermonic movement accomplishes communicative purposes with listeners. Where Craddock is clearly the builder most responsible for the contemporary prominence of the New Homiletic, Randolph was its architect, framing its implicit structure in new conceptions about the sermon's concern, its means of seeking confirmation and concretion in the lives of listeners, and the necessity

---

of Faith; idem, *Theology and Proclamation*; and Fuchs, "Must One Believe in Jesus if He Wants to Believe in God?"

5. Lowry, "Afterword," 122.
6. McClure, *Preaching Words*, 94–95.
7. Thor Hall at Duke Divinity School was first to recognize that Randolph and fellow homiletician Bill Malcomson were calling for a new homiletic movement based on the "eventfulness" of preaching. At that time Hall wanted to expand this movement to include insights from the media theory of Marshall McLuhan but his book is more theoretical than practical as a homiletic; see Hall, *Future Shape of Preaching*, xvii. McClure (Preaching Words, 94) notes that others who have substantially contributed to the contours of the movement include Fred Craddock, Charles Rice, Henry Mitchell, Eugene Lowry, and Paul Wilson.

to attend to new ways of performing scriptural intentions in a sermon's construction and its communication.[8]

Identifying the Salient Features of New Homiletic

This framework remains a useful summary of the movement's salient features. It becomes particularly evident by comparing the proposals of the two works. In *The Renewal of Preaching* and in *As One Without Authority* both Randolph and Craddock invited preachers to consider what he (or she) wished to have happen as a result of someone hearing a sermon. Both homileticians invited readers to think about what a sermon does with listeners rather than focus on what a sermon is. Randolph argued that, "Preaching is understood not as the packaging of a product but as the evocation of an *event*."[9] Both books treated preaching as *event*, as that which brings the Word of God to expression in the concrete situation of hearers.[10] Both writers considered language as a vehicle through which preacher and listener co-participate in the creation of an experience of meaning. Here the focus is not on what language says, but in the performative function of preached words communicated in living situations, in the co-creation of sermonic meaning. Both writers argue that it is through a sermon as a meaning/word event that listener and preacher can both experience the reality and possibility of the divine. This is the essence of gospel performed in Craddock's sermon, "Doxology" appended to the 1974 revision of his text and it is heart of Randolph's challenge that the concern of preaching is to discover the intentionality of a biblical text (what the text is doing just as much as what it is saying) in order to discover a way to perform an intention aligned with this "arc of action called for by the biblical word to its point of intersection with the contemporary congregation."[11]

---

8. Craddock, *As One Without Authority*. A revised edition of this book was published a few years ago (2001), but the original second edition serves as my source of historical comparison here.

9. Randolph, *Renewal* (1969), 19.

10. Ibid., Craddock argued that, "Certainly the content of communication is important, but it is in *speaking* words that an event occurs which transcends the informational dimension of the transaction. Something happens, involving at least two people, because spoken words effect participation and communication"; *As One Without Authority*, 27–28.

11. Randolph, *Renewal* (1969), 30.

Both writers turned away from older, answer-driven models of preaching in favor of discovering how to help listeners confirm the truth of the preached Word in ways less dependent on the authoritative claims of proof. Randolph was at the top of his incisive form when he claimed:

> It was a fateful day when the venerable John A. Broadus asserted, in the work that was to become the standard in its field for generations, that homiletics was a branch of rhetoric. American homiletics has not yet completely reconstituted after this stroke which severed preaching from theology and dropped it into the basket of rhetoric held by Aristotle. If the new hermeneutic can help develop the living communication between homiletics and the other theological disciplines which it both deserves and needs, we shall be grateful.[12]

This conception of confirmation shifts the focus away from argument and proofs by encouraging *kerygmatic* reasoning that is conducted by way of parable, examples, biography, autobiography, and other means to create authentication for biblical claims that would resonate with the experience of listeners.

Craddock was similarly concerned to create identification with listeners by layering a pathway that models a process of coming-to-understanding for listeners. He argued that preaching should model a process of arriving at understanding not unlike that experienced by the pastor preparing a sermon during the week. The claim of the book's title, to preach *As One Without Authority* was predicated on his argument that:

> No longer can the preacher presuppose the general recognition of his authority as a clergyman, or the authority of his institution, or the authority of Scripture . . . This condition is rapidly disappearing and the claim of the Gospel must be presented on its own terms with the understanding that the hearers stand amid several alternative . . . Unless there is room to say NO there is no room for a genuine YES. And yet it is apparent that the new situation in which preaching occurs is critical, and unless recognized by the minister and met with a new format, his sermons will at best seem museum pieces.[13]

Notice that both authors argue for *kerygmatic* rather than topical reasoning as the means of arriving at what to say in a sermon. The goal is to

---

12. Ibid., 21.
13. Craddock, *As One Without Authority*, 14–15.

imagine a relevant "process by which the meaning of the biblical text is strengthened, corroborated, and engrained *in the lives of hearers.*"[14]

Both homileticians eschewed the traditional category "application" as too heavy-handed, as too didactic. At the same time both would argue that a preacher should have in mind an appropriate range of relevant responses appropriate to the intention of a biblical claim and relevant to concrete contemporary contexts. Their two approaches to concretion of the message differ in style here. Randolph argues for both direct and indirect concretions that embody productive ways of enacting this intention. Thus, for sermons on social issues, Randolph finds that preachers typically must be more pragmatic in providing direction, helping listeners imagine possible ways of enacting a biblical truth. On the other hand he affirms that of the two approaches to concretion indirection is "the most effective way to bring texts to expression *in the long run.*"[15] Craddock is famous for proposing that sermon design should move inductively from the particularity of shared identifications of experience/meaning to affirmation(s) that re-conceive that shared identification in light of a general biblical truth.[16]

What is true for both is that preachers must find ways to express intentions that are aligned with the biblical intentions of the text rather than personally asserting authoritative claims that tell listeners what they ought to do. Craddock's argument about sermon applications follows naturally from his argument for organizing sermons inductively. Thus:

> One need not often make the applications of the conclusion to the lives of . . . hearers. If *they* have made the trip, then it is *their* conclusion and the implication for their own situations is not only clear but personally inescapable . . . For this reason, the inductively moving sermon is more descriptive than hortatory, more marked by the affirmative than the imperative, with the realization, of course, that the strongest of all imperatives is a clear affirmative that has been embraced.[17]

---

14. Randolph, *Renewal* (1969), 51.
15. Ibid., 88–89.
16. Craddock, *As One Without Authority*, 154–58.
17. Ibid., 57–58.

For both writers the drawing of conclusions should be shaped much like the logic of one of Jesus' parables in which listeners are left to their own devices to ponder "Whoa! What will I do with/make of that?"[18]

When it comes to sermon construction Craddock's natural Southern storytelling style has a predilection for narrative indirection while the assumptions behind Randolph's northern idiom are characterized by a willingness to be more direct without necessarily becoming directive. Both writers were strongly influenced by Amos' Wilder's work on the significance of biblical genres and by H. Grady Davis's claim that sermon form should somehow mirror the intention of its genre in the biblical text, that preaching an intention aligned with a biblical text may need to view textual forms as equally inspired as the content of its communication. Craddock acknowledges this, but his own commitment to an inductive form seems at times to be at odds with its implication to explore a variety of sermonic designs.[19] Randolph is more expansive in this matter, urging that "the preacher must take the literary form of the text into account" and then "seek the sermonic form which best shares the intention and mood of the text."[20]

What matters for the parallel I wish to draw here is that both writers were concerned that sermon intentions be shaped by the performative concern of the text. This was then and still is the most salient feature of New Homiletic preaching.[21] Preaching, conceived of in this manner, enacts Word of God rather than explains it. Its concentration on the 'intentionality arc' of the text and on performing intentions aligned with textual concerns is vital to the identity of this movement. The focus on viewing the sermon as an opportunity to preach in such a way as to create an experience-of-meaning for listeners rather than simply affect an experience for them is also at heart of New Homiletic preaching. Issues of form become central; especially attention to the form of the biblical text and the power by which that form communicated its message.

Brief as the influence of the European theology of the New Hermeneutic may have been, it provided Randolph, Craddock, and other New Homiletic preachers with the theological means to rescue homiletics

---

18. See Reid, *Four Voices*, 132–33.
19. Craddock, *As One without Authority*, 152–54.
20. Randolph, *Renewal* (1969), 105–6.
21. Reid, *Four Voices*, 139.

from its exile and captivity in rational argument theory and restore it to its central place as the fruition of theology properly conceived.[22]

Not long after writing *The Renewal of Preaching* Randolph returned to denominational leadership and parish ministry until the turn of the century. Craddock's *As One without Authority* went through several additions and other books that honed and developed this approach to preaching followed. For a century Broadus had set the standard that a preacher must assume the mantle of an expert making astute observations and well-crafted argument. Over time Craddock's *oeuvre* shifted this burden, helping preachers to learn how to adopt the mantle of the thoughtful sage who designs sermons in which "There can be no shock of recognition until there is first a nod of recognition."[23] In New Homiletic, it is this co-participation in the creation of an experience of meaning that embodies the notion of concretion in which the sermon provides listeners with ways of enacting a biblical truth.

In 1995 Paul Wilson turned back to Randolph's formulation of the core features of *Renewal*'s divisions to summarize what he came to see as the foundational features of New Homiletic.[24] Far from a set of museum pieces in the history of homiletics, Wilson argued that these core features are as vital today as when first articulated. Wherever preachers finally choose to surrender the burden and the battles that arise as a result of having to assume the mantle of constant expertise, they will discover the attraction of New Homiletic preaching.[25] And when they do, they will owe a dept of gratitude to Randolph and Craddock who pioneered this tidal shift in homiletic theory and practice for preaching the gospel.

From New Homiletic to Next Homiletic

My assessment above discussed the arguments of both *The Renewal of Preaching* and *As One without Authority* in the past tense, as ideas first articulated in a specific era, because I was trying to indicate how Randolph's

---

22. I address concerns with this dependence and its implications for the continued relevance of homiletics based on the *eventfulness* of preaching in the commentary below on the Communication chapter.

23. Craddock, *Preaching*, 160.

24. Paul Scott Wilson, *Practice of Preaching*, 14.

25. For an important emergent example of this burnout from the burden of modernism's expectation of pastoral expertise see McLaren, *A New Kind of Christian*; and idem, *Story We Find Ourselves In*.

division of the core conceptions of New Homiletic identified the central features that surfaced in Craddock's work a few years later. At this point I want to shift my verbs to the present tense to provide commentary on the contribution of Randolph's revision intended for a new generation of readers.[26] The present volume adds material to the original work such that Randolph hopes its version of New Homiletic will become the Next Homiletic.

The original *Renewal* proposed the core features of New Homiletic in four chapters that covered five commitments. His discussion of communication was folded into the chapter division for construction and limited the treatment to consideration of genres of biblical communication relevant to preaching.[27] In revising the original he returns to this underdeveloped theme of communication and addresses its implications, not only for sermon design, but also for every element of the *eventfulness* of preaching. As a revised edition, *The Renewal of Preaching in the 21st Century* primarily attends to the relevance of the digital culture revolution for preaching. Attention to issues of communication is now a feature of every chapter. The intervening years of his pastoral ministry and his current role as Professor in Residence of Communications at the Berkeley Graduate Theological Union's Center for the Arts, Religion and Education and his Presidency and teaching at Olivet University in San Francisco have opened Randolph's eyes to myriad ways that preaching is being conceived by a new generation of theological communicators. It is as if that last, dangling fifth division of the original book is finally being picked up and addressed at the other end of his illustrious career.

When I say the words digital revolution, I suspect that some readers may think I am speaking of the broadcast revolution, but these are quite different transformations in contemporary culture. As a communication theorist I would argue that we have many different kinds of media cultures reflected in contemporary North American Christian churches. Some congregations are still deeply tied to the oral culture; I think of deeply

---

26. It should be noted that the core features of the original *Renewal* hold up over time because New Homiletic is still with us in pulpits everywhere. McClure's dates in his *Key Terms* definition of the movement cited above should be understood with reference to development of theory supporting this movement rather than its preacherly practice.

27. Randolph had originally intended that the book should have a fifth division that would treat *Communication* in the 1969 *Renewal*, but eventually decided against it; e-mail exchange June17, 2008.

liturgical congregations here where the sermon is often but a homily in a much larger expression of worship. Some congregations are wedded to the print culture; I think of Reformation congregations here where worship bulletins are as carefully crafted as preaching manuscripts, where both documents manage the oral and verbal experience of a worship participant. The broadcast culture in congregations has seen its fullest fruition in the mega-church where the pastor preaches from outlines, employs theatrical techniques to connect with audiences, and creates dramatic moments of high audience impact more resonant in effective corporate presentational speaking than traditional preaching.[28] The emerging digital culture in the church portends the possible liminal evocation of the oral culture by reframing the past as *bricolage* for contemporary worship, by moving from broadcast's sense of event-centered relevance to the personal sense of resonance, and by shifting our notion of worship participants from listener to learner. Rex Miller has succinctly summarized how two elements of preaching differ in each of these cultures:

- *Relating to God*—Oral-Liturgical as an I-Thou dialogue, Reformation as an I-It monologue, Broadcast as They-It silence, and Digital as an I-They panalogue.

- *Revelation of God*—Oral-Liturgical as direct encounter, Reformation through Scripture, Broadcast through Scripture and experience, and Digital by immersion.[29]

As helpful as it was to turn to Ong and McLuhan at the outset of the Broadcast era, or Ellul and Postman in the midst of it, we need to turn to a new generation of theorists to contemplate the implications of the digital revolution for the church. Who these theorists will be is still in flux.

In my own modest foray into this area, at the conclusion of *The Four Voices of Preaching*, I argued that we need to shift our thinking away from the listener-centered paradigm of preaching to a learner-centered paradigm. I argued for a return to the immediacy of the oral-liturgical way of relating that also assumes the underpinnings of print and broadcast advances without assuming their ways of relating to God and the revelation

---

28. An example of this high-impact conference or corporate style of speaking adapted to the broadcast culture can be found in Wiseman, *Presenting to Win*.

29. Miller, *Millennium Matrix*, 102 and 226. For a more academic defense and discussion of these cultural divisions see Chesebro and Bertelsen, *Analyzing Media*.

of God. In the Great Commission Jesus invited his followers to go and make *learners*—not *listeners*—of all nations. In the twenty-first century people in our congregations will increasingly come to expect preachers to discover how to make sermonic learning a more collaborative venture, something that involves their imaginative commitment to remain intellectually and emotionally involved in the meaning-making process of preaching.[30]

The Renewal of Preaching (2009) provides an important roadmap that suggests ways congregants participating in Christian worship can experience the faith expressed in the sermon as vital to the digital world of daily connectivity in their lives. This homiletic will attend to the concern of this shift from listener to learner. Randolph states the prospect succinctly:

> The Next Homiletics, the homiletics that is to come in the twenty-first century, will build on the foundation secured in the twentieth century in its theological seriousness and communications creativity. It will continue in its concern for biblical message and human contact, seek connection and confirmation, be concrete, and seek effective construction and communication. Its goal will be eventfulness.[31]

Rather than proposing a model of preaching in which listeners can become passive participants of broadcast culture preaching effectiveness, Randolph keeps the focus on the eventfulness of preaching. He contends that pastoral consideration of the eventfulness of preaching should effect how the preacher thinks about a sermon from preparation to penetration.

The question is whether Randolph has simply expanded an undeveloped chapter of the previous volume in light of contemporary taste to include "new media" or has he identified an important turning point for homiletic theory yet again? If Miller is correct, that a paradigm shift in ways of being a congregation is occurring, that the Broadcast era is giving way to an emergent digital era of convergence congregations, then Randolph may have identified something central to this development as well. Miller writes:

30. Reid, *Four Voices*, 222.
31. Randolph, *Renewal* (2009), 13.

Convergence churches will develop skills to create collaborative experience. You might think of this as a techno-Quaker meeting, a jazz ensemble, or improvisational theater. All of these are highly integrative and even newcomers quickly get oriented and participate. These interactive assemblies transcend the challenge of trying to choose the right style of service—whether contemporary, traditional, youth, or blended. They will also transcend age barriers and be more inclusive of youth and elders. This happens as a result of the shift away from stage performance as the center of the event to personal interaction and group dynamics as the new center. With this new center these gatherings might be 'unplugged' or multimedia to the max.[32]

Digital consciousness churches are not print or broadcast era congregations. They are congregations transforming from a long history of being passively listener-centered parishioners now becoming learner-centered participants in worship as preaching in these congregations attends more and more to ways that worshippers are *active* co-creators of the meanings made of the sermon.[33]

In a presentation at the 2005 Academy of Homiletics I made an argument that, the urgent task of the twenty-first century pulpit is to examine the degree to which it is still dependent on an outdated theory of education for its metaphoric frame of 'learner' with reference in its theology of preaching. I argued that educational theory in the US had moved away from teacher-centered and listener-center models of learning and assess-

---

32. Miller, *Millennium Matrix*, 89–90. For the first homiletics textbook designed to give voice to this vision of a convergence church, see Pagitt's proposal of preaching as a progression dialogue; *Preaching Re-Imagined*.

33. In a 2005 paper for the Academy of Homiletics titled "From Listener to Learner: A Learner-Centered Model of Preaching," I made an argument that, "The urgent task of the 21st century pulpit is to examine the degree to which it is still dependent on an outdated theory of education for its metaphoric frame of 'learner' with reference in its theology of preaching. I wish to argue that educational theory's new metaphor of 'the learner' can serve as a productive frame of reference for contemporary homiletics—especially those homiletics interested in the role of conversation and dialogue in preaching. Homiletics' shift during the last quarter of the 20th century to a listener-centered approach to preaching and to exploring the performative nature of the biblical texts in preaching were valuable first steps toward identifying the importance of conversation and dialogue in preaching, but a further re-orientation is needed that shifts the focus from sermons shaped for listeners to sermons that make learners" (Academy Papers, 211). New Homiletic moved us from a preacher-centered to a listener-centered paradigm of preaching.

ment-driven models focused on 'the learner.' Today's learner-centered teachers and professors recognize that Internet generation students construct knowledge through gathering and synthesizing information. They are primarily interested in assignments that help them integrate learning for emerging issues and real problems. The teacher's new role is to coach and facilitate learning that happens together. The lecture has diminishing appeal in the twenty-first century. These parishioners will increasingly expect preachers to make sermonic learning a more collaborative venture. I believe homiletics' listener-centered preachers will increasingly need to shift the focus from sermons shaped for listeners to sermons that serve learners.[34] This is why I an excited by the shift in Randolph's vision. His call to integrate the digital revolution into what he envisions as Next Homiletics is in concert with my own call to see preaching—whether New Homiletic, conversational, dialogical, or Next Homiletics—become a Learner-Centered Homiletic.

A Revised Renewal and the Proposal of a Next Homiletic

In the preface of the original *Renewal* Randolph succinctly claimed that "What is crucial for homiletics is not so much what the sermon 'is' as what the sermon 'does.'"[35] And what is crucial in this revision is not so much what this focus on communication would have the sermon *be* as what it would have the sermon *become*. The introductory chapter of the revision reviews the basic argument in the original *Renewal* and then calls for a reconsideration of New Homiletic in light of the digital revolution that has made new media available for use in preaching. He reviews the original features of New Homiletic and proposes a revision of them that would support the Next Homiletic. These new features bring focus to the sermon's content and concern, its connection and confirmation, its construction and composition, its communication, and its concretion and transformation.

The central shift for Randolph's notion of sermonic Content and Concern is for preachers to develop a capacity to *visualize the text*. He challenges preachers, "With the words and images from your study recreate a vision of the people in the passage acting out their drama. This may

---

34. Reid, "From Listener to Learner," 211.
35. Randolph, *Renewal* (1969), vii.

seem extraneous at first but it is becoming increasingly recognized by Biblical scholars that much of the Bible is intrinsically and intentionally dramatic."[36] Here he develops the argument that part of the intentional process of preaching must include ways to embody the narrative qualities of the text for participants. In this chapter Randolph incorporates key ideas developed by other New Homileticians such as Charles Rice, Thomas Troeger, Paul Wilson, as well as contributions by his fellow Graduate Theological Union faculty member Doug Adams.[37] For example, Paul Wilson employs the metaphor of 'filmmaking' and challenges preachers to help worship participants visualize the text. Instead of focusing on crafting literary language, preachers are asked to think of themselves as scriptwriters tasked with making the text come alive. Wilson explores the dangers as well as the promise of this re-conception of the preacher's intentional task, but this shift focuses on the poetics of creating experiences of meaning for worship participants rather than arranging the rhetoric of argument development. This shift has become a significant indicator of New Homiletic thought. For several writers like Rice and Adams the transition is more than just one of imagination—the move is quite literally embodied in ways that the preacher enacts or performs textual implications in non-oral or extra-verbal means.

In discussing Connection and Confirmation Randolph claims that twenty-first century preaching will engage in more serious dialogue with poetics, aesthetics, and imagination as it connects with what has become a highly visual culture as opposed to our former highly print oriented culture. This will require a more significant engagement with the possibilities of new media and greater engagement with understanding communication theory as it relates to religious expression. The chapter is more evocative than specific and differs from its original by recognizing there is less of a need to refute the dominance of the cognitive rational argument models in a twenty-first century homiletic. The older cognitive, representationalist model of preaching is still alive and well, but Randolph is now far from the lone voice crying in the wilderness in challenging its assumptions. That battle has been waged. In this chapter he is more concerned to point preachers toward resources that help facilitate Confirmations. Two significant elements are explored in this revision. The first is his

---

36. Randolph, *Renewal* (2009), 33.

37. Rice, *Embodied Word*; Troeger, *Imagining a Sermon*; Wilson, *Four Pages of Preaching*; and Adams, *Eyes to See Wholeness*.

claim that, "Poetry and story have much in common, of course, and are not opposed to one another. However, there is a non-narrative element in poetry that remains largely unexplored in preaching . . ."[38] The second is his affirmation of what is now a truism: "Moving pictures are the lingua franca of our time. Everyone speaks movies."[39] Not only does film speak across cultural boundaries, but also its visual dynamic can enhance the dramatic elements inherent in biblical narrative. Randolph's attention to use of poetry and film is more suggestive than definitive, but it represents a more productive focus on the "how" of Confirmation than that found in the first edition.

In the chapter on construction and composition Randolph embraces the move toward adding LCD projected video experiences as part of the development of a sermon's design. He contends that, "In the twenty-first century, the visual element will play a larger part not only in understanding the text but in composing and communicating the sermon."[40] He points to Richard A. Jensen's *Envisioning the Word: The Use of Visual Images in Preaching* as an example of the kind of aid preachers must turn to if they want to recover a tradition that validates the movement toward employing the visual as well as the spoken word in preaching.[41] The goal is to help congregations envision using aids to accompany the spoken word to bring life to assisting worship participants in tracking with the movement of the spoken word. These may include the discrete use of PowerPoint, the use existing 'viral video' or short films from Sermon Spice.com, even the use of video clips specifically filmed to enhance the sensibility of a preacher's sermon.[42] Randolph continues to believe that the path beyond

38. Randolph, *Renewal*, 68.

39. Ibid., 71. John Lyden's argument is important here. He explores how film functions as carrier of contemporary cultural morals and values, and therefore as a way of conveying a religious worldview for those who enter is ways of being in world; hence his title; Lyden, *Film as Religion*. For more evangelically oriented approaches to film and religion see Johnston, *Reel Spirituality*; and in popular culture, see Detweiler and Taylor, *Matrix of Meanings*.

40. Randolph, *Renewal* (2009), 65.

41. Jensen, *Envisioning the Word*; see also Moore and Wilson, *Design Matters*.

42. Wikipedia indicates that "viral video" refers to "video clip content which gains widespread popularity through the process of internet sharing, typically through email or IM messages, blogs and other media sharing websites." Current popular examples at the time of this writing are Saturday night Live and MadTV Comedy sketches, and unintentionally released video clips like "The Evolution of Dance" and web productions intended for free distribution like "I Got a Crush . . . on Obama." See http://en.wikipedia

Commentary

boredom for contemporary preaching lies in understanding how to engage the hearts and minds of those participating in worship while simultaneously being hermeneutically true to pursuing an intention aligned with the concern of the text of the sermon. He notes that explorations of narrative have been particularly productive in New Homiletic preaching and that drawing on new media forms of narrativity simply enhances the interaction of narrative design in preaching. Randolph provides a wealth of examples from his own experience to elaborate ways in which use of media in worship can enhance the experience for participants.

Chapter Five on Communication begins with the claim that, "the communications revolution that is sweeping through churches around the world (is) leaving some on fire and others burned out. Preachers on fire without being burned out grasp communication as Performance, Production and Process."[43] Randolph explores his threefold division, in this order in the chapter. More significantly, this discussion of communication theory tends to reflect a semiotic, processural rather than an event-oriented approach to understanding communication theory. Here, I would offer a corrective—a critique that, if it is eventually adopted by Randolph, would strengthen rather than weaken the argument not only of the chapter and this revision but the whole book.

Most theorists of the hermeneutics of human communication tend to accept Gadamer's dictum that "Being that can be understood is language" or they may explore communication by way of the French (rather than German) tradition of European philosophical hermeneutics found in Ricoeur or Levinas.[44] They assume that language is constitutive of the *event* of being human and a human experience of reality. They reject theories of human communication that assume language mirrors reality representationally. Table 1 provides a basic comparison of the two approaches. At the heart of the matter is whether one views the expression of language between people as a process or an event.[45] This summary

---

.org/wiki/Viral_video. For Sermon Spice videos see http://www.sermonspice.com/. For an example of a preacher who regularly includes video clips to advance the sensibility of the sermon for participants see sermons by Craig Groeschel of LifeChurch.tv. A recent example can be found at http://www.lifechurch.tv/message-archive/one-prayer/2.

43. Randolph, *Renewal* (2009), 91.

44. E.g., Madison draws on both Gadamer and Ricoeur; Madison, *Hermeneutics of Postmodernity*.

45. This chart and its implications for homiletics was first presented in a paper presented at the Academy of Homiletics in 2006 titled "Dancing at the Edge of Rhetoric."

draws on the work of communication theorist John Stewart who claims "language cannot be both a *way of being* constitutive of humanity and a system instrumentally employed by already constituted humans to represent cognitions and accomplish goals."[46] Most non-semiotic theorists (by which I mean hermeneutic theorists and social constructivists) tend to view semiotic approaches to the philosophy of communication as too dependent on the conduit metaphor that privileges *process* over *event*. Hermeneutically oriented philosophers of communication tend to speak of "world" or "worlds" as the metaphor to frame understanding. Metaphors matter. And theory matters because it's implicit assumptions about the function of language in communication and its function to shape how we see world "leak out" in our everyday talk.

TABLE 1: Comparison of Semiotic and Post-Semiotic Communication Assumptions

Semiotic Focus	Post-semiotic Focus
It requires the theorist to distinguish between a linguistic and a non-linguistic world, between the world of language as signifier and some other world of mental experiences, things, ideas, concepts, etc. signified. A commitment to two worlds.	Language should be *viewed as event* rather than as a system. A commitment to language as *an event* in which meaning continually occurs.
It operates with an "atoms vs. molecules" metaphor where a linguistic world is composed of phonemes, morphemes, words, utterances, and speech acts. A commitment to atomizing.	*Communicative events* that are human presume the distinctive element of humanity as a contextual requirement: understanding. A commitment to view language as both con-textual and collaborative.

Professor Randolph was present for the discussion. The only changes I have made to the chart have been to italicize the references to the eventfulness of articulate contact with others as an alternative way of viewing communication that of a process. The chart is my own distillation of Stewart's comparison of the two philosophies of communication in Stewart, "The Symbol Model vs. Language as Constitutive Articulate Contact." Essays by a variety of post-semiotic communication theorists are included in this volume. See also Stewart, *Language as Articulate Contact*.

46. Stewart, "Editor's Introduction," 275.

It cannot avoid the subject-object dichotomy inherent in the representational claim of the symbolizing relationship between the units of these two worlds. A commitment to representationalism.	Humans constitute world and reality through languaging. A commitment to treat *a human contact event* as something participants live into by inhabiting language.
It operates with the assumption that these ontologically distinct worlds function as an operative system. A commitment to a system.	Human understanding occurs in contact between persons making it irreducibly dialogical or interpersonal. A commitment to refute 'brute data' of systems in favor of treating world as always world-for and the beings for whom it is for are relational beings.
It assumes that language thus functions as a tool to accomplish communicative ends. A commitment to a functional understanding of language as tool.	Human understanding occurs as a function of articulate contact—accomplishes differentiation paradigmatically as a result or oral-aural contact. A commitment to treat language as the primary ways humans accomplish who they are since humans *inhabit* or live in language.

The question we may wish to pose is what we should make of this continued attention to the eventfulness of language as *a commitment to treat language as the primary ways humans "accomplish" who they are since humans inhabit or live in language.* The theological hermeneutics of Ebeling and Fuchs may have become passé, but Heideggarian philosophical hermeneutics are far from passé in the hermeneutics of contemporary communication theory.[47] Philosophy of communication theorists like

---

47. It turns out that the New Hermeneutic was primarily a theology of revelation that failed to take hold as a substantive contribution to theology because it was too narrowly fixed on this one doctrinal ledge and two narrowly dependent on Heidegger. In 1969 Robert Kysar concluded that, "Language-event is a near mythical category by which the [New Hermeneutic] theologian speaks of that experience of authentic self-expression and/or communication . . . [And for this reason] It has been proposed that the new hermeneutic theology is a radically anthropocentric understanding of the theological task; it has been proposed that the revelatory referent of the experience of the language-event is really human personality," "Demythologizing the New Hermeneutic Theology," 222–23. In the current revision of *Renewal* Randolph acknowledges the limitations of this dependence on the New Hermeneutic while still affirming that "there remains truth at the heart of the claim [of preaching's *eventfulness*] that cannot be discarded"

Michael Hyde, Calvin Schrag, and John Stewart have been deeply influenced by the European philosophical hermeneutics of Heidegger and Gadamer, even as they pursue trajectories beyond these theorists.[48] In this sense, I would argue that it is still vital for preaching to consider the way in which meaning occurs as an event of coming-to-understanding as listener-learners appropriate understanding of their faith through preaching. This is central to framing the act of coming-to-understanding of one's self as an identity formed and shaped by a theological tradition appropriate understanding of their faith through preaching coming-to-understanding of one's "self" as an identity formed and shaped by a theological tradition appropriate understanding of their faith through preaching. This is central to framing the act of coming of knowing. This conception of the eventfulness of preaching is certainly part of a Heideggarian trajectory of thought taken up in Paul Ricoeur's philosophical theology of Christian proclamation:

> If we can no longer define hermeneutics as the search for another person and psychological intentions that hide behind the text, and if we do not want to reduce interpretation to the identification of structures, what remains to be interpreted? My response is that to interpret is to explicate the sort of being-in-the-world unfolded in front of the text. Here we rejoin Heidegger's suggestion about the meaning of *Verstehen*.... The moment of understanding responds dialectically to being in a situation, as the projection of our "ownmost" possibilities in those situations where we find ourselves.[49]

[per e-mail exchange]. On the influence of the New Hermeneutic on New Homiletic preaching, see Kay's review of *Renewal of Preaching in the 21st Century*. A more substantive engagement is taken up in Kay, *Preaching and Theology*, 77–104. For those who wish to understand Randolph's original degree of indebtedness to the New Hermeneutic, see Randolph, "Introduction," in *On Prayer* by Gerhard Ebeling.

48. Hyde was the keynote speaker of the National Communication Association's annual meeting of 2007. See Hyde, *Life-Giving Gift of Acknowledgement*; idem, editor, *Communication Philosophy and the Technological Age*; Jost and Hyde, eds., *Rhetoric and Hermeneutics in Our Time*; Schrag, *Communicative Praxis and the Space of Subjectivity*; Stewart, *Language as Articulate Contact*; idem, editor, *Beyond the Symbol Model*. For Jewish appropriations of Heideggarian hermeneutics one might start with Bruns, *Hermeneutics, Ancient and Modern*; and a modest starting point for a thoroughly Heideggarian theological hermeneutics would be Jeanrond, *Theological Hermeneutics*. The contemporary homiletician most influenced by this trajectory of Heideggarian-Gadamerian hermeneutics in communication theory is Bullock, *Preaching with a Cupped Ear*.

49. Ricoeur, "Philosophy and Religious Language," 43. Many ideas from essays in this volume could have been cited to indicate this trajectory of philosophical thought; consider Ricoeur's interest in Heidegger's philosophy of testimony, 108–13. For further

Commentary

And it is the projection of our "ownmost" possibilities that is also at the heart of the process of coming-to-understanding that New Homiletic preachers like Randolph and Craddock desired to see realized in their focus on the *eventfulness* of preaching.

I leave it to homiletic theologians to assess whether rhetoric's continued valuation of the eventfulness in a hermeneutic philosophy of communication might affect how one treats the double agency of the divine and human in preaching.[50] As a communication theorist, my role is draw attention to the communicative dimension of preaching. For his part, Randolph notes that homileticians must certainly beware when drawing on communication theory since the concerns "of the spiritual and transcendent" are absent in many of its theories.[51] A number of religious communication theorists recently have begun to address this void. Consider here Fortner's *Communication, Media, and Identity: A Christian Theory of Communication*, Schultze's *Christianity and the Mass Media in America*, Schultze and Woods' *Understanding Evangelical Media*, as well as my own effort to identify a theory of Christian Communication in "A Rhetoric of Christian Discourse."[52]

In the next chapter I find the strongest correlation supporting the language of my own argument that homiletics must shift its paradigm from a listener-centered to a learner-centered approach to preaching. In proposing to treat the features of concretion and transformation Randolph states:

---

development of the relationship between Ricoeurian philosophical theology and New Homiletic, see Reid, *Four Voices*, 128–32. My contention is that this connection is indirect but that developments in philosophical theology during this period such as the turn to narrative were conterminous with continuing development of thought in New Homiletic.

50. A starting place might be to consider Tracy's tensional treatment of *event* as both language event and as Divine manifestation in the Word; Tracy, "Writing."

51. Randolph, *Renewal* (2009), 82.

52. Consider here Robert S. Fortner, *Communication, Media, and Identity*; Schultze and Woods Jr., eds., *Understanding Evangelical Media*. The latter claims to be "The first book to examine the wide-ranging relationship between evangelical Christians and the media in the twenty-first century," http://www.understandingevangelicalmedia.com/. Since both books are penned by Calvin College faculty, one is left to assume that the operative word in the claim of the second book is "evangelical." See also Kraft, *Communication Theory for Christian Witness*.

> The question today is not "Is preaching transformational?" but "How is preaching transformational?" The answer I propose is that preaching is transformational through the process by which human lives individually and collectively are renewed, including the creative process by which words of the Bible are transformed from an ancient text to a contemporary message with concrete expressions.[53]

Here we see why Randolph moved the chapter on concretion from its prior location that made it a variation on confirmation to this new location in the revision. He focuses concern on the fundamental question preachers must ask in devising a sermon: "What do I want to have happen as a result of people having participated in this preaching event, having participated in constructing meaning with me in what we hear as God's Word to us today?" This is my summary of Randolph's concern that concretion be singularly focused on the transformational.

His use of the term "transformational" in this chapter comes as a result of having grappled with Lucy Rose's assessment of his contribution to homiletic theory in her book *Sharing the Word: Preaching in the Roundtable Church*. Rose points out that she initially came to understand preaching's possibilities through the work of New Homiletic theorists. One need only look to her essay "The Parameters of Narrative Preaching" to see a model of her own process of coming-to-understanding as she sought to comprehend the homiletics of Craddock and Lowry.[54] In *Sharing the Word*, however, she explains how she came to reject these New Homiletic approaches because they have transformation of the individual in view. She was one of the first writers who attempted to shift the assumptions of preaching away from its suasory concern to affect a transformation of listeners. In challenging New Homiletic theorists she asked, "Will preachers who seek to perform texts, create new realities, or transform the worshipper be honest that their presentations of texts, new realities, and gospel values, worldviews or ways of being in the world are constructs reflecting their own biases?"[55] She rejected the implicit hierarchy that such a preaching posture adopts in favor of moving preaching into the realm of conversation as a kind of disclosive personal and confessional narrative. Preachers like Randolph do not believe a preacher can escape the per-

---

53. Randolph, *Renewal* (2009), 87–88.
54. Rose, "Parameters of Narrative Preaching."
55. Rose, *Sharing the Word*, 110.

Commentary

formative demands of biblical texts. But Rose was concerned that such a presumption risks marginalizing people and even tyrannizing them based on unperceived, or worse, reified prejudices.[56] Post-liberal, neo-Barthian, and revisionist-conversational preaching homileticians have also come to question whether New Homiletic tends to reduce and thereby limit God as One who meets worshippers at their point of need.[57]

For his part, Randolph remains committed to the relationship of calling for concretions and the need for transformation as a response to preaching. He writes: "The transformational stone rejected by some in the establishment has become the cornerstone of revolutionary preaching in the twenty-first century. Church leaders across the theological and political spectrum recognize we must be transformed by the power of God and worship and preaching are powerful instruments of love and justice. To conform to this world of war, poverty, disease and ignorance and violence is not an option for churches, individuals, groups and nations."[58] This embrace of the notion of transformation is clearly fixed in the notion of preaching's *eventful* expression as a language event of Word of God but is less open to the challenge of being a therapeutic-oriented approach to preaching precisely because he believes that New Homiletic or Next Homiletics preaching must be willing to challenge worshippers to take up and perform the concerns of love and justice which transcend the limits of the individual's own needs.

His inclusiveness in this chapter might surprise many. He finds value in the communicative strategies of both Joel Osteen and Rick Warren and Martin Luther King Jr. My quibble with this list is that it still attends more to preachers operating out of a broadcast paradigm.

In his conclusion, Randolph identifies the features that would comprise his vision of the Next Homiletics: commitment, concern, connection, confirmation, construction, communication, and commission. Apparently 'concretion' and 'transformation' have been reduced to 'commission,' quite probably driven by his tendency to prefer alliteration in

---

56. See Reid, *Four Voices*, 149–51, for this specific challenge to New Homiletic preaching.

57. See McClure, *Preaching Words*, 95. McClure's discussion in this brief assessment treats post-liberal and neo-Barthian responses to New Homiletic, but is less clear on the subject of revisionist analysis of the intersection between the human and the divine in "what language performs."

58. Randolph, *Renewal* (2009), 92.

chapter titles. The notion of commission—"Send the people forth into the world and go with them" probably represents a fair summary of his belief that the performative claims of the biblical text enacted in a sermon will always call for response that involves repentance in having missed God's mark for human purposes and the challenge to take action when we have sensed the truth of a biblical claim performed in the sermon.

Next Homiletic—Digital or Dialogical?

Whether this revised version of Next Homiletics features will be accepted by those like Lowry, who contend that Randolph had initially named "the room beyond the door" is yet to be seen. They have their own vision of that 'room.' In fact, revising a seminal text forty years later is so unusual that it is more likely that it would be a new generation that would have to be willing to take up this revised vision than the generation who first embraced it. What matters here is not just Randolph's desire to justify the continued relevance of a movement which he helped birth, but his consistent willingness to re-imagine the portion of the original revolution that could not be resolved until a broadcast culture began to give way to the digital culture.

What he has done is to provide a substantive argument for why New Homiletic's frame of reference is more amendable to the exploration of the implications of this sea change in contemporary worship and preaching practices. It is yet to be seen whether this model or another will take hold. Randolph remains committed to his belief that the original revolution still matters and those who believe that scripture makes performative claims on those who would preach its message may agree.

As I write these words, I have been in email conversation with Professor Ronald Allen of Christian Theological Seminary in Indianapolis. In commenting on an insight about preaching by a working pastor, he observed, "In theology, the seminary is usually 25 years ahead of the church. But in practice, the church is usually quite a few years ahead of the seminary, especially when the church's practice deviates from 'tradition.'"[59] Those who know Prof. Allen can hear the cadence of his voice in the way that idea is phrased. I mention this astute observation at this point to say that when Randolph first penned *Renewal* he was on the cusp of entering that "25 years ahead of the church." What we have here may simply be a

---

59. Email correspondence sent to the author by Ronald Allen, June 17, 2008.

good word on the other end of that curve, or a resituating of the first paradigm for an emerging paradigm 25 years later. Time and faithful practice in the churches will be the true judge.

Can New Homiletic become Next Homiletic by embracing rather than resisting the digital revolution? Whatever the answer to that question may be, it is intriguing to see David Randolph still imagining the possibilities of renewal for another generation forty years later.

Works Cited

Adams, Doug. *Eyes to See Wholeness: Visual Arts Informing Biblical and Theological.* Prescott, AZ: Educational Ministries, 1995.

Bruns, Gerald L. *Hermeneutics, Ancient and Modern.* New Haven: Yale University Press, 1992.

Bullock, Jeffrey F. *Preaching with a Cupped Ear: Hans-Georg Gadamer's Philosophical Hermeneutics as Postmodern Wor(L)D.* Berkeley Insights in Linguistics and Semiotics. New York: Lang, 1999.

Chesebro, James W., and Dale A. Bertelsen. *Analyzing Media: Communication Technologies as Symbolic and Cognitive Systems.* London: Guilford, 1996.

Craddock, Fred B. *As One without Authority: Essays on Inductive Preaching.* 2nd ed. Enid, OK: Phillips University Press, 1974.

———. *As One without Authority: Revised and with New Sermons.* St. Louis: Chalice, 2001.

———. *Preaching.* Nashville: Abingdon, 1985.

Detweiler, Craig, and Barry Taylor. *A Matrix of Meanings: Finding God in Pop Culture.* Grand Rapids: Baker Academic, 2000.

Ebeling, Gerhard. *The Nature of Faith.* Translated by Ronald Gregor Smith. Philadelphia: Fortress, 1961.

———. *Theology and Proclamation: Dialogue with Bultmann.* Translated by John Riches. Philadelphia: Fortress, 1966.

———. *Word and Faith.* Translated by James Leitch. Philadelphia: Fortress, 1963.

Eslinger, Richard. *A New Hearing: Living Options in Homiletical Method.* Nashville: Abingdon, 1987.

Fortner, Robert S. *Communication, Media, and Identity: A Christian Theory of Communication.* The Communication, Culture, and Religion Series. New York: Rowman & Littlefield, 2007.

Fuchs, Ernst. "Must One Believe in Jesus if He Wants to Believe in God?" *Journal for Theology and the Church* 1 (1965) 147–68.

Hall, Thor. *The Future Shape of Preaching.* Philadelphia: Fortress, 1971.

Hogan, Lucy Lind, and Robert Stephen Reid. *Connecting with the Congregation: Rhetoric and the Art of Preaching.* Nashville: Abingdon, 1999.

Hyde, Michael J., editor. *Communication Philosophy and the Technological Age.* University: University of Alabama Press, 1982.

———. *The Life-Giving Gift of Acknowledgement.* Philosophy/Communication Series. West Lafayette, IN: Purdue University Press, 2005.

Jeanrond, Werner G. *Theological Hermeneutics: Development and Significance.* New York: Crossroad, 1991.
Jensen, Richard A. *Envisioning the Word: The Use of Visual Images in Preaching.* Fortress Resources for Preaching. Minneapolis: Fortress, 2005.
Johnston, Robert K. *Reel Spirituality: Theology and Film in Dialogue.* Engaging Culture. Grand Rapids: Baker Academic, 2000. 2nd ed., 2006.
Jost, Walter, and Michael J. Hyde, editors. *Rhetoric and Hermeneutics in Our Time: A Reader.* Yale Studies in Hermeneutics. New Haven: Yale University Press, 1997.
Kay, James F. *Preaching and Theology.* Preaching and Its Partners. St. Louis: Chalice, 2007.
———. Review of *The Renewal of Preaching in the 21st Century* in *The Princeton Seminary Bulletin* 20.3 (1999) 353–54.
Kraft, Charles H. *Communication Theory for Christian Witness.* Rev. ed. Maryknoll, NY: Orbis, 1991.
Kysar, Robert. "Demythologizing the New Hermeneutic Theology." *Journal of the American Academy of Religion* 37 (1969) 215–23.
Lowry, Eugene L. "Afterword." In *The Homiletical Plot,* 117–32.
———. *The Homiletical Plot: The Sermon as Narrative Art Form.* Rev. ed. Louisville: Westminster John Knox, 2001.
Lyden, John C. *Film as Religion: Myths, Morals, and Religion.* New York: New York University Press, 2003.
Madison, G. B. *The Hermeneutics of Postmodernity: Figures and Themes.* Studies in Phenomenology and Existential Philosophy. Bloomington: Indiana University Press, 1988.
McClure, John S. *Preaching Words: 144 Key Terms in Homiletics.* Louisville: Westminster John Knox, 2007.
McLaren, Brian D. *A New Kind of Christian: A Tale of Two Friends on a Spiritual Journey.* San Francisco: Jossey-Bass, 2001.
———. *The Story We Find Ourselves In: Further Adventures of a New Kind of Christian.* San Francisco: Jossey-Bass, 2008.
Miller, M. Rex. *The Millennium Matrix: Reclaiming the Past, Reframing the Future of the Church.* San Francisco: Jossey-Bass, 2004.
Moore, Jason, and Len Wilson. *Design Matters: Creating Powerful Imagery for Worship.* Nashville: Abingdon, 2006.
Pagitt, Doug. *Preaching Re-Imagined: The Role of the Sermon in Communities of Faith.* Grand Rapids: Zondervan, 2005.
Randolph, David James. "Introduction." In *On Prayer: Nine Sermons* by Gerhard Ebeling, 1–36. Philadelphia: Fortress, 1966.
———. *The Renewal of Preaching.* Philadelphia: Fortress, 1969.
———. *The Renewal of Preaching in the 21st Century.* 1st ed. Introduction by Robert Stephen Reid. New York: Hanging Gardens, 1998.
Reid, Robert Stephen. "Dancing at the Edge of Rhetoric." Paper presented at the Academy of Homiletics 2005.
———. "Exploring Preaching's Voices from *Ex Cathedra* to Exilic." In *Preaching the Eighth Century Prophets,* edited by David Fleer and Dave Bland. Rochester College Lectures on Preaching 5. Abilene, TX: ACU Press, 2004.
———. *The Four Voices of Preaching.* Grand Rapids: Brazos, 2006.
———. "From Listener to Learner: A Learner-Centered Model of Preaching." Paper presented and archived in the 2005 Academy Homiletics Papers.

———. "Introduction." In *The Renewal of Preaching in the 21st Century* by David James Randolph, 1–12.

———. "Postmodernism and the Function of the New Homiletic in Post-Christendom Congregations," 1–13.

———. "A Rhetoric of Christian Discourse." *Journal of Communication and Religion* 31 (Fall 2008) forthcoming.

Reid, Robert Stephen, Jeffrey Bullock, and David Fleer "Preaching as the Creation of an Experience: The Not-So-Rational Revolution of the New Homiletic." *Journal of Communication and Religion* 18.1 (1995) 1–9.

Rice, Charles. *The Embodied Word: Preaching as Art and Liturgy*. Fortress Resources for Preaching. Minneapolis: Fortress, 1991.

Ricoeur, Paul. "Philosophy and Religious Language." In *Figuring the Sacred: Religion, Narrative, and Imagination*, 35–47. Translated by David Pellauer. Edited by Mark I. Wallace. Minneapolis: Fortress, 1995.

Rose, Lucy Atkinson. "The Parameters of Narrative Preaching." In *Journeys toward Narrative Preaching*, 24–47. New York: Pilgrim, 1990.

———. *Sharing the Word: Preaching in the Roundtable Church*. Louisville: Westminster John Knox, 1997.

Schrag, Calvin O. *Communicative Praxis and the Space of Subjectivity*. Studies in Phenomenology and Existential Philosophy. Bloomington: University of Indianapolis Press, 1989.

Schultze, Quintin J., and Robert H. Woods Jr., editors. *Understanding Evangelical Media: The Changing Face of Christian Communication*. Downers Grove: InterVarsity, 2008.

Stewart, John, editor. *Beyond the Symbol Model: Reflections on the Representational Nature of Language*. SUNY Series in Speech Communication. Albany: State University of New York Press, 1996.

———. "Editor's Introduction." In *Beyond the Symbol Model*, 1–6.

———. *Language as Articulate Contact: Toward a Post-Semiotic Philosophy of Communication*. SUNY Series in Speech Communication. Albany: State University of New York Press, 1995.

———. "The Symbol Model vs. Language as Constitutive Articulate Contact." In *Beyond the Symbol Model*, 9–63.

Tracy, David. "Writing." In *Critical Terms for Religious Studies*, edited by Mark C. Taylor, 383–93. Chicago: University of Chicago Press, 1998.

Troeger, Thomas H. *Imagining a Sermon*. Abingdon Preacher's Library. Nashville: Abingdon, 1991.

Wilson, Paul Scott. *The Four Pages of Preaching: A Guide to Biblical Preaching*. Nashville: Abingdon, 1999.

———. *The Practice of Preaching*. Nashville: Abingdon, 1995. Rev. ed., 2007.

Wiseman, Jerry. *Presenting to Win: The Art of Telling Your Story*. Updated ed. Upper Saddle River, NJ: Pearson/Prentice Hall, 2006.

Bibliography

Adams, Doug. *Eyes to See Wholeness: Visual Arts Informing Biblical and Theological Studies in Education and Worship through the Church Year.* Prescott, AZ: Eb Educational Ministries, 1995.

Arndt, William F., and F. Wilbur Gingrich. *A Greek-English Lexicon of the New Testament and Other Early Christian Literature.* 2nd ed. Chicago: University of Chicago, 1979.

Auerbach, Erich. *Mimesis.* Translated by Willard Trask. Garden City, NY: Doubleday, 1957.

Augustine. *On Christian Doctrine.* Translated by D. W. Robertson. New York: Macmillan, 1958.

Baehr, Ted. *So You Want To Be In Pictures?* Nashville: Broadman & Holmann, 1995.

Barrett, David, and Todd Johnson. *World Christian Trends AD 30–AD 2200: Interpreting the Annual Christian Megacensus.* Pasadena, CA: William Carey Library, 2001.

Bewer, Julius. *The Literature of the Old Testament.* New York: Columbia University Press, 1933.

Bowra, Maurice. *Heritage of Symbolism.* New York: St. Martin's, 1943.

Broadus, John. *On The Preparation and Delivery of Sermons.* New York: Armstrong & Son, 1870. (The 1870 edition remains definitive of Broadus himself and is the work referred to in this book. Later revisions bring this work into different contexts while subtracting from and adding to the original work.)

Brueggemann, Walter. *Finally Comes the Poet: Daring Speech for Proclamation.* Minneapolis: Fortress, 1989.

Buechner, Frederick. *The Magnificent Defeat.* San Francisco: Harper & Row, 1985.

Buttrick, David. *Homiletic: Moves and Structure.* Philadelphia: Fortress, 1987.

Campbell, Charles L. *The Word before the Powers: An Ethic of Preaching.* Louisville: Westminster John Knox, 2002.

Cardenal, Ernesto. *The Psalms of Struggle and Liberation.* Translated by Emile G. McAnany. New York: Herder & Herder, 1971.

Cherry, Richard L. et al., editors. *A Return to Vision.* 2nd ed. Boston: Houghton Mifflin, 1974.

Childers, Jana. *Performing the Word: Preaching as Theatre.* Nashville: Abingdon, 1998.

Colapinto, John. "The Interpreter." *The New Yorker*, April 16, 2007; online: www.newyorker.com.

Craddock, Fred B. *As One Without Authority: Essays on Inductive Preaching.* 2nd ed. Enid, OK: Phillips University Press, 1974.

———. *Preaching.* Nashville: Abingdon, 1985.

Dillenberger, Jane. *The Religious Art of Andy Warhol.* New York: Continuum, 1998.

Bibliography

———. *Style and Content in Christian Art*. New York: Abingdon, 1965.
Dodd, C. H. *According to the Scriptures*. London: Nisbet, 1952.
———. *The Parables of the Kingdom*. Rev. ed. New York: Scribner, 1961.
Eason, Tim. *Media Ministry Made Easy: A Practical Guide to Visual Communication*. Nashville: Abingdon, 2003.
Farrer, Austin. *A Rebirth of Images: The Making of St. John's Apocalypse*. 1949. Reprinted, Eugene, OR: Wipf & Stock, 2007.
Fraoli, James O. *Storyboarding 101: A Crash Course in Professional Storyboarding*. Studio City, CA: Michael Wise Productions, 2000.
Funk, Robert W. "How Do You Read? A Sermon on Luke 10:25–37." *Interpretation* 18 (1964) 56–61.
———. *Language, Hermeneutic, and Word of God: The Problem of Language in the New Testament and Contemporary Theology*. New York: Harper & Row, 1966.
———. "The Old Testament in Parable." *Encounter* 26 (1965) 251–67. Reprinted in *Language, Hermeneutic, and Word of God*, 199–223.
———. *The Poetics of Biblical Narrative*. Foundations and Facets. Sonoma, CA: Polebridge, 1988.
Gladwell, Malcolm. *The Tipping Point: How Little Things Can Make a Big Difference*. New York: Little, Brown, 2002.
Hauerwas, Stanley, and William H. Willimon. *Resident Aliens: Life in the Christian Colony*. Nashville: Abingdon, 1992.
Hogan, Lucy Lind, and Robert Reid. *Connecting with the Congregation: Rhetoric and the Art of Preaching*. Nashville: Abingdon, 1999.
Hoy, David Couzens. *The Critical Circle: Literature, History and Philosophical Hermeneutics*.
King, Jr., Martin Luther. *Strength to Love*. New York: Walker, 1984.
Kuhn, Thomas S. *The Structure of Scientific Revolutions*. 3rd ed. Chicago: University of Chicago Press, 1996.
Madgalene, David. "God the Cruiser." In *I Heard A Journeyman Sing/Yo escuché el canto del caminante*, 110–12. Albany, CA: New Way Media, 2005.
McClure, John S. *The Four Codes of Preaching: Rhetorical Strategies*. Louisville: Westminster John Knox, 2003.
———. *Preaching Words: 144 Key Terms in Homiletics*. Louisville: Westminster John Knox, 2007.
———. *The Roundtable Pulpit: Where Leadership & Preaching Meet*. Nashville: Abingdon, 1995.
Melville, Herman, *Moby Dick*. New York: Norton, 2002.
Michalson, Carl. *The Hinge of History*. New York: Scribners, 1959.
Miles, Margaret R. *Image as Insight: Visual Understanding in Western Christianity and Secular Culture*. 1985. Reprinted, Eugene, OR: Wipf & Stock, 2006.
Minear, Paul S. *Images of the Church in the New Testament*. 1960. Reprinted, New Testament Library. Louisville: Westminster John Knox, 2004.
Niebuhr, H. Richard. *Christ and Culture*. New York: Harper, 1951.
Niebuhr, Reinhold. *Faith and History*. New York: Scribner, 1951.
Obama, Barack. *The Audacity of Hope*. New York: Three Rivers, 2006.
Oden, Thomas C., editor. *Ancient Christian Commentary on Scripture*. Downers Grove, IL: InterVarsity, 1998.
O'Donnell, James J. *Augustine: A New Biography*. New York: Ecco, 2005.

Bibliography

Osteen, Joel. *Your Best Life Now: 7 Steps to Living at Your Full Potential*. New York: Faith Words, 2007.
Randolph, David James. "Augustine's Theology of Preaching." PhD dissertation, Boston University, 1962.
———. *Candles in the Dark, Flames for the Future: Preaching and Poetry in Times of Crisis*. Editor. Albany, CA: New Way Media, 2003.
———. *On the Way after 9/11: New Worship and Art*. Albany, CA: New Way Media, 2002.
———. *The Power That Heals: Love, Healing & Trinity*. Nashville: Abingdon, 1994.
———. *The Renewal of Preaching*. Philadelphia: Fortress, 1969.
———. *The Renewal of Preaching in the 21st Century*. Babylon, NY: Hanging Gardens, 1998.
Rauschenbusch, Walter. *Christianity and the Social Crisis in the 21st Century: The Classic that Woke up the Church*. New York: HarperOne, 2007.
Reid, Alistair. "Growing, Flying, Happening." In *Oddments, Inklings, Omens, Moments*. Boston: Atlantic-Little, Brown & Co., 1958.
Reid, Robert Stephen. "An Introduction." In *The Renewal of Preaching in the 21st Century*, 1–12. Babylon, NY: Hanging Gardens, 1998.
———. *The Four Voices of Preaching*. Grand Rapids: Brazos, 2006.
———. "Postmodernism and the Function of the New Homiletic in Post-Christendom Congregations." *Homiletic* 20.2 (1995) 1–13.
———. "Preaching as the Creation of an Experience: The Not-So-Rational Revolution of the New Homiletic." *The Journal of Communication and Religion* 18 (1995) 1–9.
———. "A Rhetoric of Contemporary Christian Discourse." *Journal of Communication and Religion* 31 (Fall 2008).
Rice, Charles L. *The Embodied Word: Preaching as Art and Liturgy*. Minneapolis: Fortress, 1991.
Rose, Lucy Atkinson. "The Parameters of Narrative Preaching." In *Journeys toward Narrative Preaching*, edited by William B. Robinson, 24–47. New York: Pilgrim, 1990.
———. *Sharing the Word: Preaching in the Roundtable Church*. Louisville: Westminster John Knox, 1997.
Rush, Michael. *New Media in Late 20th Century Art*. World of Art. London: Thames & Hudson, 1999.
Sittler, Joseph Sittler. *The Ecology of Faith*. Philadelphia: Muhlenberg, 1959.
Stidger, William L. *Preaching Out of the Overflow*. Nashville: Cokesbury, 1929.
Sweet, Leonard. *Aquachurch*. Loveland, CO: Group Publishing, 1999.
———. *SoulTsunami: Sink or Swim in New Millennium Culture*. Grand Rapids: Zondervan, 1999.
Thorson, Esther, and David W. Schumann. *Internet Advertising: Theory and Research*. No city: Psychology Press, 2007.
Troeger, Thomas H. *Ten Strategies for Preaching in a Multimedia Culture*. Nashville: Abingdon, 1996.
Van Seters, Arthur. *Preaching as a Social Act: Theology and Practice*. Nashville: Abingdon, 1988.
Vier, Peter, OFM. *Evidence and Its Function according to John Duns Scotus*. St. Bonaventure, NY: Franciscan Institute, 1951.
Wagner, William. *How Islam Plans to Change the World*. Grand Rapids: Kregel, 2004.

Bibliography

Wallace, James A. *Preaching to the Hungers of the Heart: The Homily on the Feasts and within the Rites.* Collegeville, MN: Liturgical, 2002.

Wallis, Jim. *The Great Awakening: Reviving Faith and Politics in a Post-Religious Right America.* New York: HarperOne, 2008.

Ward, Richard F. *Speaking from the Heart: Preaching with Passion.* Nashville: Abingdon, 1992.

Warren, Rick. *The Purpose-Driven Church: Growth without Compromising Your Message and Mission.* Grand Rapids: Zondervan, 1995.

———. *The Purpose-Driven Life: What on Earth Am I Here For?* Grand Rapids: Zondervan, 2002.

Wilder, Amos N. *The Language of the Gospel.* New York: Harper & Row, 1964.

Wilken, Robert Louis, editor. *The Church's Bible.* Grand Rapids: Eerdmans, 2003.

Wilson, Paul Scott. *The Practice of Preaching.* Nashville: Abingdon, 1995.

Wink, Walter. *Engaging the Powers: Discernment and Resistance in a World of Domination.* The Powers 3. Minneapolis: Fortress, 1992.

———. *Naming the Powers: The Language of Power in the New Testament.* The Powers 1. Minneapolis: Fortress, 1984.

———. *The Powers that Be: Theology for a New Millennium.* New York: Doubleday, 1999.

———. *Unmasking the Powers: The Invisible Forces that Determine Human Existence.* The Powers 2. Minneapolis: Fortress, 1986.

———. *When the Powers Fall: Reconciliation in the Healing of Nations.* Minneapolis: Fortress, 1998.

www.ingramcontent.com/pod-product-compliance
Lightning Source LLC
Chambersburg PA
CBHW031457160426
43195CB00010BB/1008